FACT or FAKE?

To my two youngest grandchildren,
Ella and Dash Gorospe, with the hope that on their life's journey,
they will always honor, love, and pursue the truth.

— A.Z.

FACT or FAKE?

Test Your Smarts!

Allan Zullo

Scholastic Inc.

ISBN 978-0-545-53551-9

12 11 10 9 8 7 6 5 4 3 14 15 16 17 18/0

Printed in the U.S.A. 23

First edition, December 2013

The publisher thanks the following for their kind permission to use their photographs in this book:

Photographs © 2013: Alamy Images/Shotshop GmbH: 139; AP Images: 47 (fls), 193 (Metropolis Collectibles), 45; Biosphoto: 19 (J.-L. Klein & M.-L. Hubert), 23 (Jim Zipp/Ardea); Dreamstime: 95 (Crazy80frog), 27 (Dzombie), 25 (Ecophoto), 81 (Jeffstein), 11 (Jmaentz), 109 (Johnnycheuk), 163 (Mckown), 7 (Mirceax), 77 (Photoeuphoria), 129 (Photowitch), 43 (Rabbit75), 31 (Stevebyland), 161 (Sumnersgraphicsinc), 147 (Tiler84); Fotolia: 145 (Africa Studio), 187 (aris sanjaya), 159 (Diane Keys), 13 (Dogs), 59 (Erica Guilane-Nachez), 133 (freshidea), 127 (Guido Vrola), 33 (Marco Regalia), 113 (shinnji); Getty Images: 205 (General Photographic Agency/Stringer), 21 (Jeffrey Coolidge), 191 (Jim Spellman/WireImage), 143 (Rubberball/Mark Andersen); iStockphoto: 17 (bucky_za), 137 (cdascher), 75 (CHKnox), 197 (cornishman), 111 (DNY59), 79 (fototrav), 151 (Funwithfood), 117 (GlobalStock), 185 (kalimf), 155 (katra), 35 (kreicher), cover background (iStockphoto/yurok), 165 (Lauri Patterson), 173 (liveslow), 131 (lucato), 171 (Maica), 201 (NoDerog), 39 (pastorscott), 9 (Syldavia); Library of Congress: 203 (The Strobridge Lith Co., Cinti - N.Y.), 51, 53; NASA: 83 (F. Hasler, M. Jentoft-Nilsen, H. Pierce, K. Palaniappan, and M. Manyin/NASA Goddard Lab for Atmospheres - Data from NOAA), 89 (JPL/Space Science Institute), 67 (LANCE/EOSDIS Rapid Response), 55, 87, 91; Shutterstock, Inc.: 63 (enciktat), 103 (feiyuezhangjie), 15 (Hollygraphic), 65 (John A Davis), 177 (Kiselev Andrey Valerevich), cover bottom left, back cover top right (Leigh Prather), 169 (LesPalenik), 99 (LilKar), 57 (pavila), 153 (Pressmaster), 29 (Ryan M. Bolton), 107 (Samot), 105 (sjgh), 37 (Susan Law Cain), 69 (Todd Shoemake), 41 (Victorian Traditions/J.L.G. Ferris/Wolf & Co), 73 (warin keawchookul); Superstock, Inc.: 175 (ClassicStock.com), 101 (Library of Congress/Science Faction); Thinkstock: 93 (Brand X Pictures), 119 (Comstock), 123 (Design Pics), 199 (Digital Vision), 61 (Dorling Kindersley RF), cover bottom right, cover top right, cover top left, back cover top left, back cover bottom, 71, 97, 115, 121, 125, 141, 149, 157, 167, 181, 189 (iStockphoto), 179 (Lifesize), 49 (Photodisc), 135 (Purestock), 183, 195 (Stockbyte); US Air Force: 85.

CONTENTS

TRUE or FALSE?

WITCHES WERE BURNED AT THE STAKE IN MASSACHUSETTS. . . . THE MOON WILL EVENTUALLY CRASH INTO THE EARTH. . . . YOU SHRINK A LITTLE BIT EVERY DAY.

You hear statements like these all the time that make you wonder, *Is it true or is it false?* This book will help answer that most common of questions. And it will test your knowledge on subjects from animals and science to geography and beyond. Each page gives a statement, and it's up to you to decide whether it's fact or fiction. You'll find the answer on the following page.

We hope you'll have fun learning whether the statement is a proven truth—or an "urban legend" (something that's not actually true). For a fun challenge, keep track of how many statements you correctly decide are either fact or fake. Then turn to page 208 to see how your score measures up!

To get you started, here's a True fact: Of the first three sentences in this introduction, only one of the statements is, in fact, a fact. Can you guess which one?

READ ON and FIND OUT!

ANIMALS

The deadliest creatures on earth are **MOSQUITOES**.

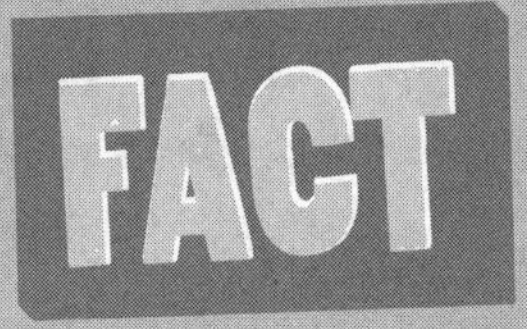

Although they're tiny and live for only a few weeks, mosquitoes cause more human suffering than any other animal on the planet.

MOSQUITOES TRANSMIT DISEASES TO ALMOST SEVEN HUNDRED MILLION PEOPLE ANNUALLY, RESULTING IN MORE THAN ONE MILLION DEATHS EVERY YEAR. The vast majority of these deaths are from malaria. The World Health Organization estimates that between 650,000 and 900,000 people—mostly African children—die annually from this mosquito-transmitted disease.

There are about 3,500 species of mosquitoes, including about 200 in North America. But not every kind of mosquito is to blame for such misery. Public Enemy No. 1 is the female *Anopheles* mosquito. She's capable of transmitting the potentially deadly malaria virus through a single bite.

Mosquitoes can also carry dengue and yellow fevers, West Nile virus, encephalitis, elephantiasis, canine (dog) heartworm, and equine (horse) encephalitis.

ATTACK DOGS

Dogs aren't always man's best friend. Sometimes there are killers among the 78 million owned canines and unknown number of strays in the United States. According to a twenty-year study by the Centers for Disease Control and Prevention, an average of sixteen people a year die from dog attacks. Here are the top five purebreds involved in the most human fatalities during the period:

- Pit bull, 66
- Rottweiler, 37
- German shepherd, 17
- Husky-type, 15
- Malamute, 12

BULLS go wild when they see the color red.

Bulls are color-blind, so it doesn't really matter what color cape is waved at them. All they see is a dark gray cloth.

FOR BULLFIGHTING, THE ANIMALS ARE TESTED FOR AGGRESSIVENESS AROUND THE AGE OF THREE. The meanest ones are brought to the bull ring. When the bull enters the ring, he gets stabbed in the back of the neck, which makes him steaming mad by the time the matador begins waving a cape in front of him. The flapping cloth is so annoying to the bull that he charges it.

So why use a red cape when any color will do? Well, red has been a tradition since the 1700s, especially in Spain, where bullfighting is the national sport. The color was chosen because it's attractive to the fans in the stands—and also hides any blood. The other side of the cape is yellow to make it more decorative. Because of his color blindness, the bull would charge just as hard at the yellow side if it was waved in front of him.

FACT or FAKE?
If you sneak up on a certain breed of GOAT and scare them, they will collapse on the spot.

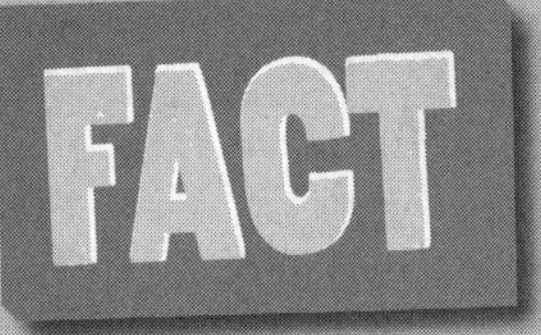

Yelling "Boo!" can tip over Tennessee fainting goats.

THE NAME IS SOMEWHAT MISLEADING BECAUSE, ALTHOUGH THESE GOATS TOPPLE OVER WHEN THEY'RE STARTLED, THEY DON'T ACTUALLY LOSE CONSCIOUSNESS. Tennessee fainting goats have a genetic condition called *myotonia*, which causes their muscles to stiffen when they get frightened or excited. This stiffening, which lasts about ten to fifteen seconds, often causes them to lose their balance, so they fall over.

The goat is not having a seizure or suffering any pain. It's just that the goat's knees are locked or, in some cases, its body completely stiffens until it falls over. Young goats tend to "faint" more than their parents. Older goats learn to spread their legs or lean against something when startled. Sometimes they continue to run about in an awkward, stiff-legged shuffle.

FACT or FAKE?

THE **BLOODHOUND** HAS THE BEST SENSE OF SMELL OF ANY CREATURE ON EARTH.

The bear has the best sense of smell of any animal on Earth.

THE BLOODHOUND IS THE BEST AMONG ITS FELLOW CANINES AT SNIFFING OUT SCENTS. But the floppy-eared dog, known for its great ability to track lost people and escaping prisoners, can't match the bear when it comes to smelling things.

The average dog's sense of smell is a hundred times keener than a human's, and a bloodhound's is three times that of the typical dog. But a bear's sense of smell is seven times better than a bloodhound's, which means the bruin's nose is 2,100 times as keen as yours.

The average bear has a highly developed nose with hundreds of times more surface area and receptorsthan a human's.

Bears' acute sense of smell helps them find food and mates, keep track of their cubs, and avoid danger. This sense is so amazing they can detect prey up to forty miles away and animal carcasses three miles away, from upwind. Bears can even notice a human scent hours after a hiker has walked along a trail.

UNBEARABLE SITUATION

The next time you camp in bear country, make sure you hang your food high up in a bear-resistant bag or airtight canister at least one hundred yards away from your shelter. Keep your tent and sleeping bag free of any lingering food odors. Otherwise, you might have an unbearable situation.

FACT or FAKE?

CROCODILES are crybabies.

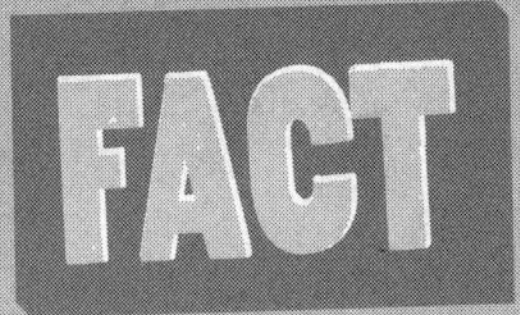

Crocodiles really do get teary-eyed when they rip their prey to shreds.

BUT IT'S STRICTLY FOR BIOLOGICAL RATHER THAN EMOTIONAL REASONS, ACCORDING TO A UNIVERSITY OF FLORIDA STUDY. When crocs eat, moisture collects in the corners of their eyes and runs down their face just like you'd expect a tear to run down your face.

In the study, captive alligators and caimans—two animals closely related to crocs—were conditioned to eating on dry land, where researchers saw the animals "cry" during most meals. Researchers say the weeping may be a byproduct of the hisses and huffs that crocs make while dining. This behavior forces air though the reptiles' sinuses, which stimulates fluid in the tear glands. These tears tend to lubricate and protect the eyes.

CROCODILE TEARS

Centuries ago, people assumed crocodiles were actually crying while killing and eating their prey. This led to the belief that crocs were shedding false tears of guilt. This assumption became the origin for the term we use today to mean a phony or insincere display of sadness. When we think someone is faking grief or pretending to cry, we say they are crying "crocodile tears."

FACT or FAKE?

The **ELEPHANT** can't jump.

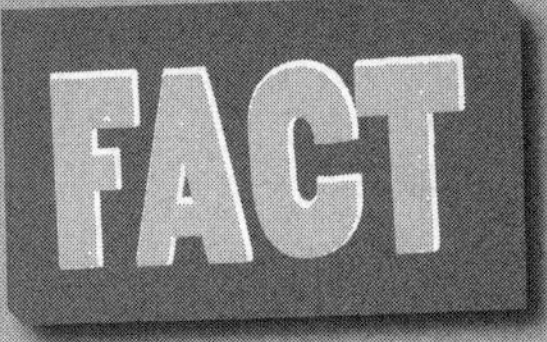

The big animal can't leap with all four feet off the ground from a stationary position.

BUT IT'S NOT ALONE IN ITS INABILITY TO JUMP. THE SAME IS TRUE FOR TWO OTHER HEAVY-WEIGHTS—THE RHINOCEROS AND HIPPOPOTAMUS. And let's not forget the sluggish sloth, which is physically unable to jump, but, given its nature, probably wouldn't leap even if it could.

As for the mature elephant, it can't jump because it weighs too much to support landing on all fours. Its legs are designed for strength rather than leaping ability. The bones in an elephant's foot are more closely packed together than other mammals', so the bones don't have the flexibility or springiness that would enable the elephant to jump.

There is little reason for an elephant to jump in its natural habitat, because it has no natural enemies (other than human poachers and hunters). Pachyderms can lose their balance easily, so they tend to walk carefully and deliberately and wouldn't think about leaping, especially when they can walk around or through an obstacle.

FACT or FAKE?

PENGUINS are polar bears' favorite meal.

Polar bears in the wild have never seen a penguin, let alone eaten one.

THAT'S BECAUSE POLAR BEARS LIVE FAR UP IN THE NORTHERN HEMISPHERE, WHILE PENGUINS GENERALLY LIVE FAR SOUTH, IN ANTARCTICA.

Almost all penguins are found in the Southern Hemisphere. The farthest north penguins naturally live is in the Galápagos Islands, on the equator, more than five hundred miles west of Ecuador. Polar bears, which are the world's largest land predators, can be found in the wild only in the Arctic Circle, including Alaska, Canada, Russia, Denmark, Greenland, and Norway. Today, twenty to twenty-five thousand polar bears roam the Arctic.

When polar bears are on land during the summer, they eat berries and plants and sometimes small mammals and birds. During the winter, they hunt for their favorite meal—the ringed seal, which is the most common seal in the Arctic region. The average ringed seal, which has a dark coat with silver rings on its back, is about five feet long and weighs between 110 and 150 pounds. Polar bears need to eat an average of one seal every four or five days to stay healthy.

DID YOU KNOW?

The word *arctic* comes from the Greek word for "bear," and *antarctic* comes from the Greek meaning the opposite, or "without bear."

FACT or FAKE?

MOTHS are attracted to bright, artificial lights.

Moths are fluttering around your porch light more out of confusion than attraction.

JUDGING BY HOW OFTEN MOTHS FLY AROUND ARTIFICIAL LIGHT, YOU'D THINK THEY WOULD FIND IT IRRESISTIBLE. But they don't. Moths find such light disorienting, according to researchers.

Lepidopterists (a fancy word for moth and butterfly scientists) believe that many kinds of moths rely on the night sky for navigational clues. For example, the insects use the moon as a reference point so they know which way is up and down and can orient themselves in a given direction.

But technology has confused moths, because they end up orienting themselves to artificial lights, which are often brighter than the moon. When moths get closer to the light, it appears to them to be moving. Because the moon is so much farther away, it seems stationary, which makes them think they've started turning the wrong way. So, they turn toward the light to get back into what they think is a straight line. As a result, they tend to circle the artificial light over and over again.

SO WHY DO MOTHS REMAIN CLOSE TO A LIGHT SOURCE ONCE THEY HAVE REACHED IT? AMONG THE THEORIES:

- Moths simply tire themselves out, so they quit flying and rest on nearby objects.
- Having reached a brightly lit spot, moths are tricked into thinking the sun is out and settle in to sleep.
- The bright lights temporarily blind the insects.

FACT or FAKE?

BATS are blind as . . . well . . . bats.

All bats can see, many of them really well, even in dim light.

THE FRUIT-EATING BAT HAS LARGE, BULGING EYES THAT HELP IT NAVIGATE, AVOID OBSTACLES, AND LOCATE FOOD BY SIGHT. But the typical insect-eating bat tends to "see" at night with its ears. It relies on echolocation—the ability to locate objects using sound. The bat sends out high-pitched sounds, usually through its mouth but sometimes through its nose. These sounds reflect off nearby objects such as trees and insects and send back echoes that help the bat determine what and where these things are.

If you see bats soaring and diving at dusk, you won't hear them use echolocation, because this high-frequency ultrasound is beyond the range of human hearing. Only through a special device can biologists detect bat calls, which average from thirty to three hundred pulses per second.

Whether they thrive on fruit or insects, all bats still use their eyesight for dodging large objects, determining their altitude, and finding their way.

GOING BATTY

- Bats are the only mammals that can fly.
- A single brown bat can catch more than a thousand small insects in an hour.
- Some bats can live to be thirty years old.
- About 25% of all the mammal species in the world are bats.
- There are more than 1,200 species of bats.

FACT or FAKE?
The GIRAFFE can go without water longer than a camel can.

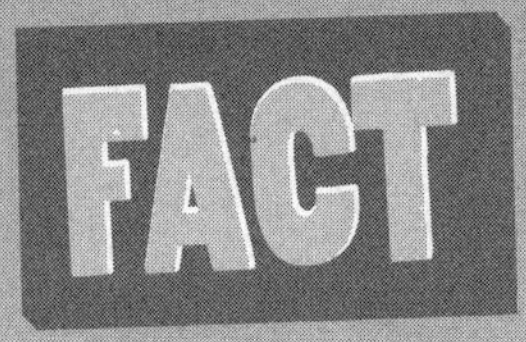

The giraffe can go for weeks without drinking water, which is much longer than a camel can.

THE LONG-LEGGED GIRAFFE GETS MOST OF ITS WATER FROM THE PLANTS IT EATS, ALLOWING IT TO AVOID DANGEROUS WATERING HOLES WHERE ITS TWO BIGGEST PREDATORS, THE LION AND THE CROCODILE, LURK. By staying away from these places as much as possible, the giraffe improves its chances for survival. Drinking water isn't as vital to the giraffe as it is for other animals.

The camel can go a week or more without water, but not as long as a giraffe. The funny-looking giraffe is able to avoid dehydration that would kill most other creatures because of its efficient red blood cells.

And, no, the camel's hump is not a water reservoir. It's just a big mound of fat and flesh. But it does serve an important role when the camel is in the middle of the desert carrying a four-hundred-pound load. The fat in the hump gets absorbed as nutrition when food is scarce.

WHO NEEDS WATER?

The kangaroo rat can live without drinking any water at all. This small mammal — which is neither a kangaroo nor a rat — is found in dry places such as the Sonoran Desert in Arizona, California, and Mexico.

It has a body chemistry that converts food, such as seeds and grains, into water. As a result, this creature, which got its name because it's a rodent that hops, doesn't need to drink water to survive. It can manufacture its own.

FACT or FAKE?

Mama **BIRDS** will reject their babies if you touch them.

Mama birds will *not* reject their babies if you touch them.

YOU'VE PROBABLY BEEN WARNED THAT IF YOU SEE A BABY BIRD HOPPING ON THE GROUND AFTER FALLING OUT OF ITS NEST, YOU SHOULDN'T PUT IT BACK BECAUSE THE MAMA BIRD WILL DETECT A HUMAN SCENT ON THE FLEDGLING AND ABANDON IT. Well, such thinking is for the birds.

Most birds cannot smell well enough to detect a human scent. The myth was started to prevent well-meaning people from putting baby birds back into nests while the little ones were learning to fly. Scientists and researchers handle baby birds all the time without mama birds abandoning them.

A mama bird might leave her baby temporarily if a human has too much contact with the fledgling, but it's not because she smells a human. It's because she might fear that she is in danger of losing her life. But generally, mama birds will fight to the death to protect their young.

Another reason the mama bird might disappear for a short time is to find more food for the baby, or to watch from a distance as the fledgling learns how to fly.

Although you shouldn't go around touching birds in nests, if you find a fallen bird on the ground, it's okay to pick it up and put it back.

FACT or FAKE?
OSTRICHES BURY THEIR HEADS IN THE SAND.

Ostriches don't bury their heads in the sand.

IF THEY DID, THEY WOULDN'T BE ABLE TO BREATHE AND THEY WOULD DIE. This myth comes from the illusion created when ostriches dig. Their heads are so small that they look like they are under the surface.

Typically, the male ostrich digs a large hole up to eight feet wide and three feet deep in the sand for the nest. The hole is deep enough that predators can't see the eggs from just a few feet away. The male and female take turns sitting on the eggs and blending into the background. During the incubation period, the ostrich will turn the eggs with its beak several times a day. From a distance, it looks as though the bird has his or her head in the sand.

If a predator approaches, the ostrich abandons the nest and flees. But not because it's a scaredy-cat. By bolting, the ostrich tries to divert the predator away from the eggs and instead chase after the big bird. Because the ostrich can run at sustained speeds of up to 40 miles per hour, most predators are left in the dust . . . and the eggs are safe.

FACT or FAKE?

HUMMINGBIRDS can't walk.

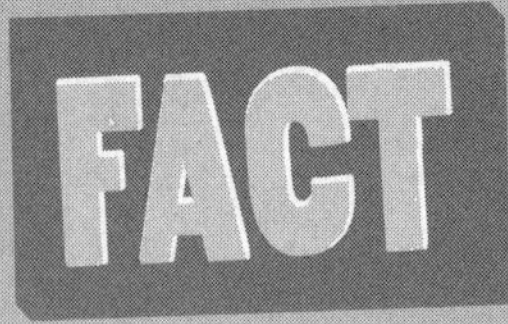

Hummingbirds can't walk.

ALTHOUGH THOSE CUTE, COLORFUL, TINY BIRDS HAVE FEET TO PERCH, THEY DON'T USE THEM TO WALK BECAUSE THEIR FEET ARE SO POORLY DEVELOPED.

Hummers spend most of their time in flight, so they seldom need to walk. After all, they can fly right, left, up, down, backward, and even upside down. They also can hover by flapping their wings in a figure-eight pattern, so why bother walking?

Their name comes from the humming noise they make by flapping their wings, which can be as fast as eighty times per second. They have a long, tapered bill that collects nectar from the center of flowers, licking up food with their tongue at more than ten licks a second. The birds also survive on tree sap, insects, and pollen. Although they are small, hummers require an enormous amount of food each day because of their incredibly fast breathing rate and heartbeat.

WALKING ON AIR

Among the birds that can't walk are:

- Ruby-throated hummingbirds
- Chimney swifts
- Swallow-tailed kites
- Belted kingfishers

FACT or FAKE?

RICE will cause birds' stomachs to explode.

It's a bird-brained myth that rice will cause birds' stomachs to explode.

MANY WEDDING PARTIES WON'T TOSS RICE AT THE BRIDE AND GROOM FOR FEAR THAT BIRDS WILL EAT IT, CAUSING THEIR STOMACHS TO EXPAND UNTIL OUR FEATHERED FRIENDS EXPLODE. But birds often eat grains like rice, wheat, and barley as part of their regular diet without any harm. Migrating birds, including ducks and geese, often consume rice from the fields on their northward journey during the spring. Blackbirds by the thousands swoop down on newly sown rice fields and consume large amounts of the kernels without any ill effects.

The myth took on a life of its own in 1988 when the popular Ask Ann Landers column published a letter from a reader who warned against throwing rice at weddings to protect birds. A few months later, Cornell ornithologist (a fancy word for bird expert) Steven C. Sibley debunked the myth in a letter that the column published. In it, he said, "There is absolutely no truth to the belief that rice (even instant) can kill birds. . . . Rice is no threat to birds. It must be boiled before it will expand. Furthermore, all the food that birds swallow is ground up by powerful muscles and grit in their stomachs."

FACT or FAKE?

HISTORY

GEORGE WASHINGTON

wore a set of hippopotamus ivory teeth.

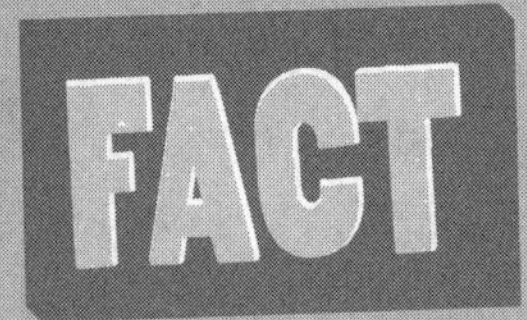

George Washington had false teeth made of hippopotamus ivory.

WASHINGTON BEGAN LOSING HIS TEETH WHEN HE WAS IN HIS TWENTIES BECAUSE HE SUFFERED FROM POOR DENTAL HYGIENE WHILE GROWING UP. He wore several dentures over the years, but contrary to popular belief, he never had a set of wooden teeth.

There are four surviving sets of Washington's choppers, which were made from eighteen-carat gold, HIPPO ivory, and lead, as well as teeth from humans (including a few of his own) and teeth from horses and donkeys. The plates of the dentures were bolted to hold them in place and had springs on them so he could open and close his mouth.

The upper and lower gold plates of Washington's dentures were connected by springs that pushed the plates against the upper and lower ridges of his mouth to hold them in place. Washington had to forcefully close his jaws to make his teeth bite together. If he relaxed, his mouth would pop open.

Maybe the reason why the Father of Our Country always looks so stern in his portraits is that he was just trying to keep his mouth closed.

FACT or FAKE?

In CONGRESS, July 4, 1776.

The unanimous Declaration of the thirteen united States of America,

Our **INDEPENDENCE** was declared on July 4, 1776.

Independence Day should have been July 2, 1776, since that's the day the Continental Congress actually declared its independence from Great Britain.

THAT EVENING, THE *PENNSYLVANIA EVENING POST*, A NEWSPAPER IN PHILADELPHIA, ANNOUNCED, "THIS DAY THE CONTINENTAL CONGRESS DECLARED THE UNITED COLONIES FREE AND INDEPENDENT STATES." John Adams wrote at the time that July 2 would be remembered in the annals of American history and would be marked with fireworks and celebrations.

Well, he was half right.

Thomas Jefferson wrote the first draft of the Declaration of Independence, which was then edited by Adams and Benjamin Franklin. Jefferson took their edits and incorporated them into what would become the final version, which was dated and adopted on July 4. In a rare historic occurrence, the document announcing independence overshadowed the event itself, and July 4 became the day that officially marked the birth of a new nation.

Americans didn't begin celebrating their independence until July 8, when the Continental Congress threw a big party in Philadelphia, including a parade. George Washington's army, which was camped near New York City, heard the news on July 9 and celebrated then. Although the document was dated July 4, the final signature of the 56 delegates wasn't penned until August 2. As for the British, they didn't learn about the declaration until August 30!

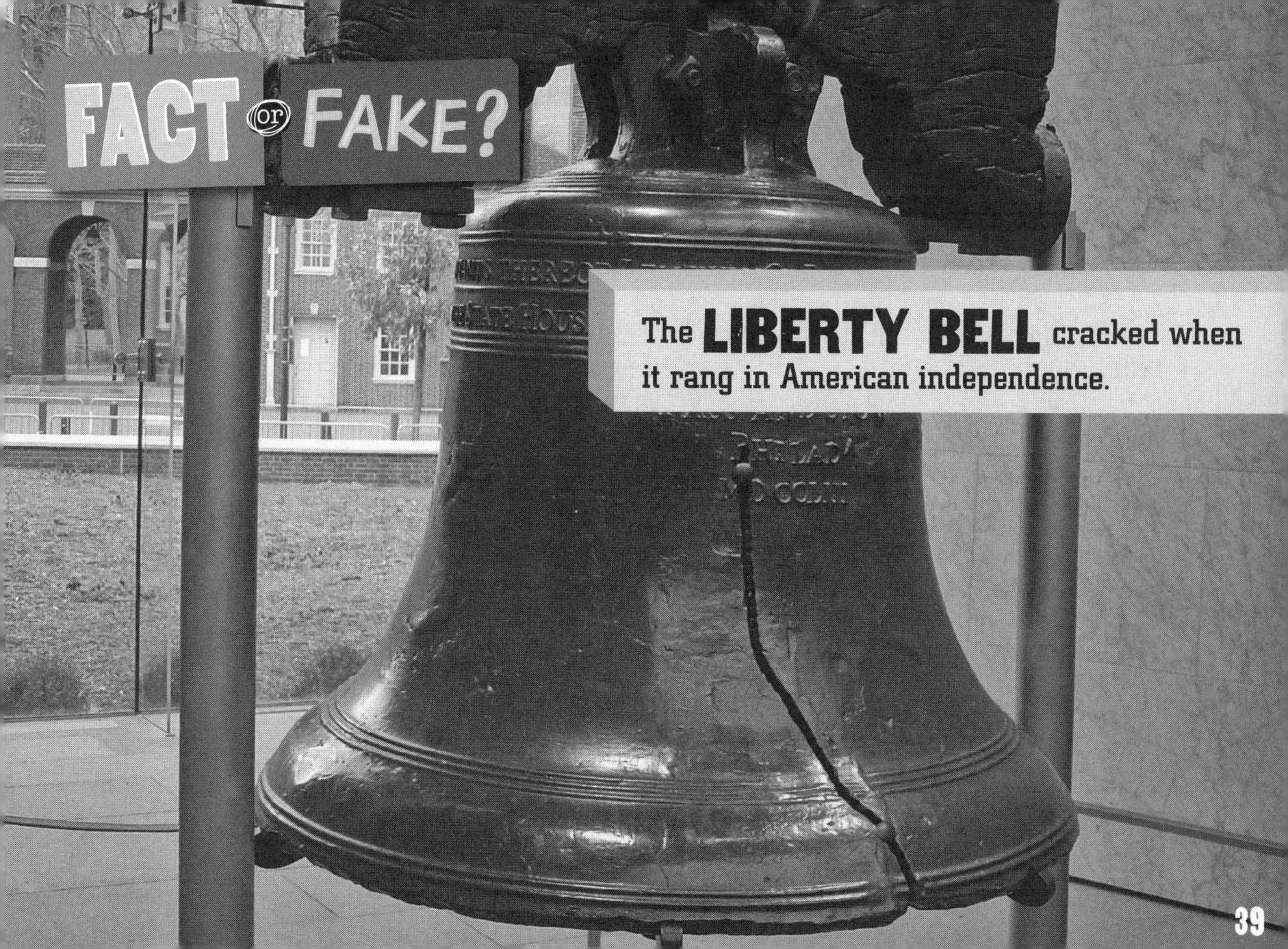

FACT or FAKE?

The **LIBERTY BELL** cracked when it rang in American independence.

The Liberty Bell did not crack while ringing in our country's independence.

YOU MAY HAVE HEARD THE OLD STORY: A YOUNG BOY WAITED OUTSIDE THE DOOR OF INDEPENDENCE HALL. As soon as he heard that independence had been declared, he signaled to an old man, who then rang the Liberty Bell so hard it cracked. It makes for a good tale. And that's all it is—a good tale, because it never happened.

The story was entirely made up by writer George Lippard, who, in 1847, wrote a fictional account of the declaration for the *Saturday Courier* about the boy, the old man, and the bell. When it came to history, Lippard had a reputation for writing about not what actually happened, but what he thought *should* have happened.

Up until then, the bell wasn't anything special. It had been cast in England in 1751 to serve in the Pennsylvania statehouse. Due to flaws in the bell when it arrived in Pennsylvania, it was melted down and recast locally in 1753. The bell, along with nearly a dozen others, was reportedly rung on July 8, 1776, when the Declaration of Independence was read to the people of Philadelphia.

It was first called the Liberty Bell in 1839 by abolitionists—people who opposed slavery—when they began using it as a symbol of their movement.

FACT or FAKE?

PRESIDENTS John Adams and Thomas Jefferson died within hours of each other on the Fourth of July.

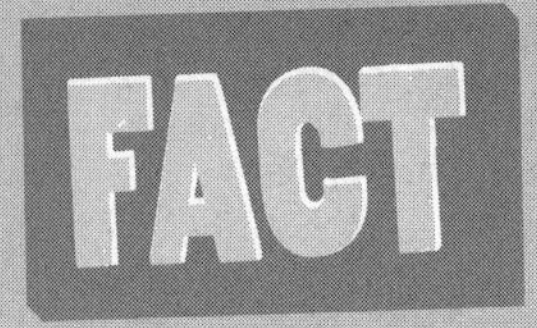

By remarkable coincidence, two presidents died on July 4, 1826.

JOHN ADAMS, THE SECOND PRESIDENT OF THE UNITED STATES, AND THOMAS JEFFERSON, THE THIRD PRESIDENT, BOTH DIED EXACTLY FIFTY YEARS TO THE DAY AFTER THE ADOPTION OF THE DECLARATION OF INDEPENDENCE.

They were among the last surviving members of the original American revolutionaries who had stood up to the British Empire and forged a new political system. They shared many similarities. Both were highly educated, became members of their colonial legislatures, were named delegates to the Continental Congress, served on the committee to draft the Declaration of Independence, became foreign diplomats, and eventually were each elected president of the United States.

On the country's fiftieth birthday, Adams (ninety), and Jefferson (eighty-two), passed away. While on his deathbed in Quincy, Massachusetts, Adams reportedly uttered, "Jefferson still lives." But the truth was that Jefferson had died five hours earlier at his home, known as Monticello, near Charlottesville, Virginia.

DID YOU KNOW

- James Monroe, our country's fifth president, also died on the Fourth of July, but in 1831, in Richmond, VA.
- Calvin Coolidge, America's thirtieth president, was born on the Fourth of July in 1872 in Plymouth, VT.

FACT or FAKE?

Native Americans sold **MANHATTAN** for $24 worth of beads.

Manhattan was sold for more than some nearly worthless beads.

IN 1626, THE LENAPE TRIBE TRADED THE ISLAND OF MANHATTAN TO THE DUTCH FOR AXES, IRON KETTLES, AND WOOL CLOTHING, RATHER THAN A FEW DOLLARS' WORTH OF BEADS, AS MANY PEOPLE BELIEVE. The Native Americans were smart traders and wouldn't have been fooled by worthless trinkets.

It was still a great deal for the colonists. Peter Minuit, director of the Dutch colony of New Netherland (which today includes parts of New York, New Jersey, Delaware, and Connecticut), bought Manhattan in exchange for goods valued at sixty guilders. The approximate value in today's currency is about one thousand dollars, according to the Institute for Social History of Amsterdam.

There is no evidence that either party in the Manhattan deal believed they had been swindled. In fact, both expected to benefit from it. The Lenape tribe hoped the Dutch would become military allies against rival Indian nations. In addition to obtaining a settlement at Manhattan, the Dutch expected the deal would secure future trading and business with the Native Americans.

FACT or FAKE?

WITCHES were never burned at the stake in seventeenth-century Massachusetts.

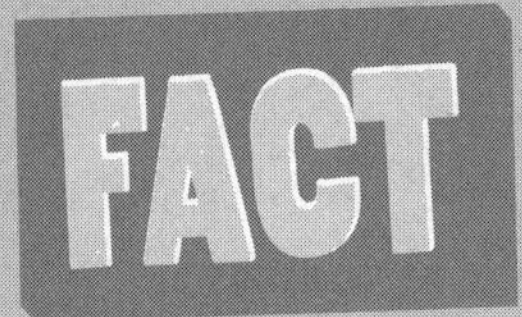

During the anti-witch hysteria of 1692-1693 in Massachusetts, no persons convicted of witchcraft were burned at the stake.

AT THE TIME, MORE THAN TWO HUNDRED PEOPLE WERE ACCUSED OF WITCHERY AND BROUGHT TO TRIAL. Twenty of them—fourteen women and six men—were convicted and executed. Nineteen were hanged and one, a seventy-one-year-old man, was crushed by rocks.

For reasons that historians still can't pinpoint, people in and around the town of Salem began fearing for their lives, convinced that many of their fellow citizens were witches bent on doing harm. Because people back then believed that children were natural witch-finders, kids were encouraged to report anyone who acted strange. Within a year, more than two hundred villagers and farmers were tried for practicing witchcraft. Historians believe many of the so-called "witches" were physically or mentally ill, or had been hallucinating from eating tainted rye bread or poison mushrooms.

The accused were kept behind bars while waiting for their day in court. Five of them died in jail due to the poor conditions. Because they were tortured, some confessed and had their lives spared, but were stripped of their property and legal rights. Witchcraft was considered a crime against the government and a felony punishable by hanging in English law, which Massachusetts followed because it was still a British colony at the time. The condemned "witches" were taken on carts to Gallows Hill, where they were hanged.

FACT or FAKE?

zzie Borden took an **AXE** and gave her mother forty whacks.
nd when she saw what she had done, she gave her father forty-one.

Despite the famous poem, Lizzie Borden was brought to trial and found innocent of the axe murders of her father, who was hacked eleven times, and her stepmother, who was hacked nineteen times.

THE GRUESOME SLAYINGS OCCURRED ON AUGUST 4, 1892, IN THE HOME OF LIZZIE'S FATHER, ANDREW, WHO WAS A WEALTHY BUT TIGHTFISTED BANKER, AND HER STEPMOTHER, ABBY. Lizzie, a thirty-two-year-old unmarried church secretary and Sunday-school teacher, visited the house and discovered the bodies. Because she had a rocky relationship with her dad and stepmom, authorities investigated Lizzie. Although they never found the murder weapon or any bloody clothes, they learned that Lizzie had burned a dress shortly after the murders. She told them she destroyed the dress after she got paint on it. The police also discovered she had tried to buy poison shortly before the killings. Lizzie explained she wanted it to clean a sealskin coat. Despite this flimsy evidence, Lizzie was arrested and brought to trial in 1893.

The case attracted widespread newspaper coverage across the country. During her three-week trial, Lizzie was portrayed as a cold, calculating killer by the prosecution, but because it was all circumstantial evidence, the jury returned a verdict of not guilty. Lizzie, who changed her name to Lizbeth, remained in Fall River until her death in 1927. Regardless of her claims of innocence, she will always be remembered in rhyme as a murderess.

FACT or FAKE?

Thomas Edison did not invent the **LIGHTBULB.**

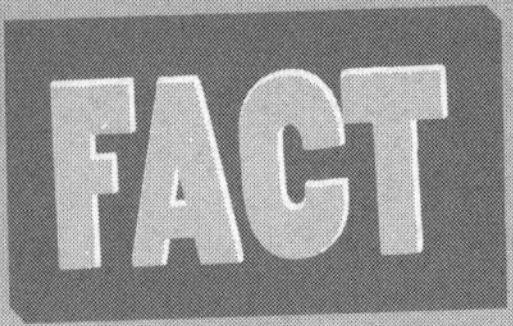

Lightbulbs had been around for more than forty years before Thomas Edison patented his much more practical version for home use.

IN 1809, ENGLISHMAN HUMPHRY DAVY DEMONSTRATED A POWERFUL ELECTRIC LAMP TO THE ROYAL INSTITUTION OF SCIENCE. The lamp produced its illumination by creating a blinding electric spark between two charcoal rods, but it was too impractical.

In 1879, British inventor Joseph Swan showed off his carbon filament lightbulb in Newcastle, England. Swan published his findings and designs in *Scientific American*. After reading the article, Edison came up with a vastly improved lightbulb and received a U.S. patent later that year.

Although Edison didn't invent the lightbulb, he made it functional. Building off the successes and failures of others, Edison was credited with inventing an electric lighting system that contained all the elements necessary to make the incandescent light practical, safe, and economical for everyday use.

INVENTIVE INVENTOR

Thomas Edison held more than one thousand patents. Among his inventions:

- Electric vote recorder (1868)
- Automatic telegraph system (1872)
- Electric pen (1876)
- Phonograph (1877)
- Motion-picture camera (1891)
- Fluorescent electric lamp (1896)
- Nickel-iron-alkaline storage battery (1900)

FACT or FAKE?

Alexander Graham Bell invented the **TELEPHONE.**

Alexander Graham Bell did not invent the telephone. A poverty-stricken Italian immigrant beat him to it.

BORN IN 1808, ANTONIO MEUCCI STUDIED DESIGN AND MECHANICAL ENGINEERING IN FLORENCE, ITALY. He moved to New York City in 1850 to develop what he called the "teletrofono." Ten years later, he held a public demonstration of his invention, which was reported in New York's Italian-language press.

Because Meucci struggled to find financial backing and didn't master English, he failed to secure a U.S. patent for his "talking telegraph." He sent a model and technical details to the Western Union telegraph company but couldn't win a meeting with executives. In 1874, he asked for the return of his materials but was told they had been lost. Two years later, Alexander Graham Bell, who had worked in a laboratory that Meucci had used as well, filed a patent for a telephone and then made a lucrative deal with Western Union. Meucci sued, but he died in 1889 before he could find justice.

At best, Bell expanded upon the knowledge and work of Meucci's invention.

FACT or FAKE?

Henry Ford invented the modern **AUTOMOBILE.**

Henry Ford was a trendsetter in the new automobile industry, but he didn't invent the car.

IN 1885, MORE THAN TEN YEARS BEFORE FORD PATENTED HIS AUTOMOBILE, KARL BENZ OF MANNHEIM, GERMANY, INVENTED A VEHICLE WITH AN INTERNAL COMBUSTION ENGINE. Unaware of Benz's efforts, another German inventor, Gottlieb Daimler, also created a similar gasoline-powered automobile at the same time.

Both Germans built compact engines containing cylinders that helped create heat-producing reactions to power their vehicles. In 1926, the two men's companies merged and began producing cars called Mercedes-Benz.

What Henry Ford did was revolutionize the automobile industry by creating the Model T Ford, an affordable, easy-to-drive vehicle that was introduced in 1908. As head of the Ford Motor Company, he created an assembly line of well-paid workers who mass-produced the cars, and forever changed the way automobiles were manufactured and sold.

THE FIRST CAR

Nicolas Joseph Cugnot built the first self-powered vehicle for the road in 1769 in France. However, his invention was powered by steam rather than gasoline, and didn't have an internal combustion engine. Cugnot drove his contraption in Paris at the reckless speed of 2.5 miles an hour. His invention is recognized by the British Royal Automobile Club and the Automobile Club de France as being the first car.

FACT or FAKE?

The Soviet Union was the first country to land a **SPACECRAFT** on the moon.

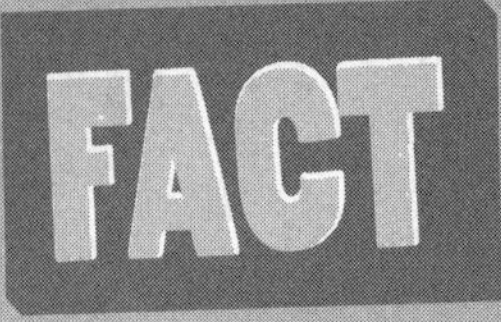

The Soviet Union's Luna 2 was the first spacecraft to reach the moon when it crash-landed on the lunar surface on September 14, 1959.

EARLIER, LUNA 1, THEN KNOWN AS THE FIRST COSMIC SHIP BY THE SOVIETS, WAS ON ITS WAY TO THE MOON WHEN A MALFUNCTION CAUSED AN ERROR IN THE ROCKET'S BURN TIME. The spacecraft missed the moon by 3,725 miles. Not until February 1966 did the Russians land a spacecraft safely on the moon, with Luna 9.

Four months later, on June 2, 1966, the United States landed its first spacecraft, Surveyor 1, softly on the lunar surface. The mission was considered a success and demonstrated the technology necessary to achieve a safe landing. On July 20, 1969, Neil Armstrong, commander of the Apollo 11 mission, became the first human to set foot on the moon.

SPACED OUT

Here are some things invented through NASA research that ended up becoming common everyday items:

- Water filters
- Cordless tools
- Safety grooves on runways and roads
- Adjustable smoke detectors
- Shoe insoles
- Scratch-resistant eyeglasses
- Invisible braces

FACT or FAKE?

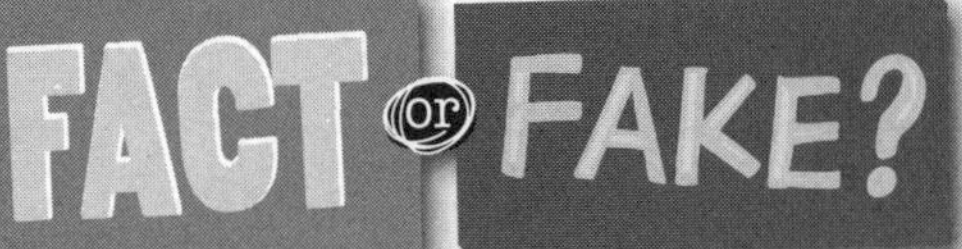

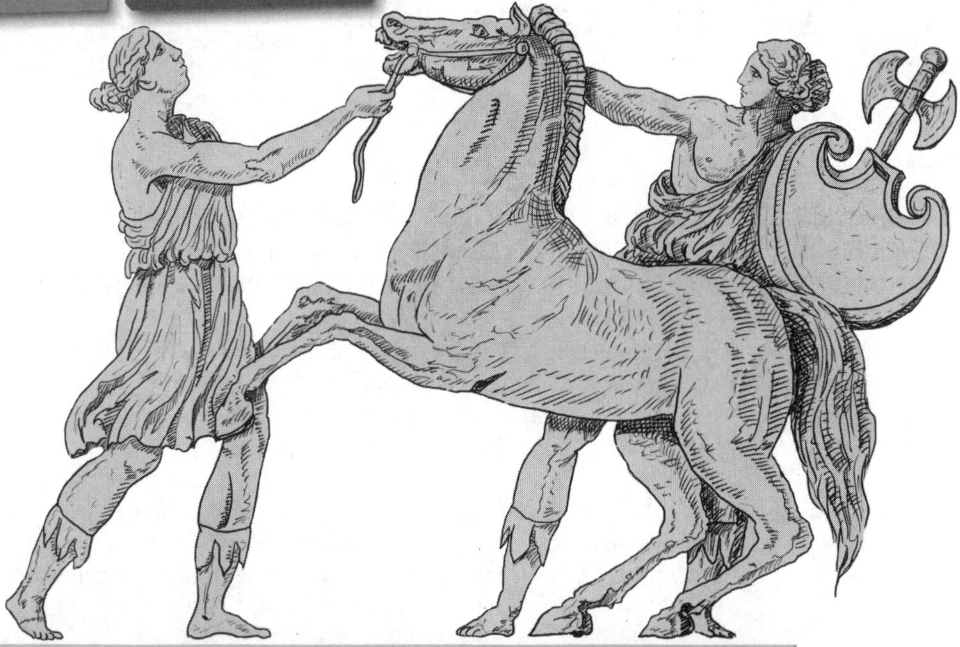

Some **GLADIATORS** in ancient Rome were women.

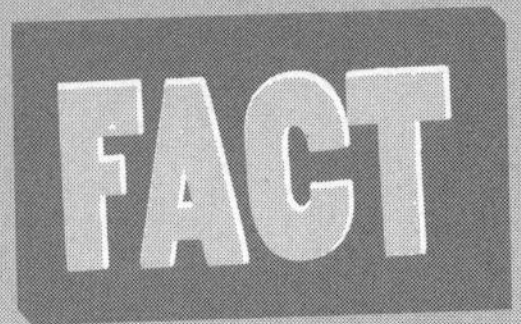

The first documented appearance of gladiatrices—female gladiators—appeared under the reign of Nero (born 37 CE, died 68 CE).

LIKE THEIR MALE COUNTERPARTS, THESE WOMEN WERE ARMED FIGHTERS WHO ENGAGED IN VIOLENT COMBAT WITH HUMANS AND ANIMALS FOR THE ENTERTAINMENT OF AUDIENCES IN ARENAS THROUGHOUT THE ROMAN EMPIRE.

Drawings and sculptures show that the gladiatrices rarely wore helmets or chest protectors. A second-century Roman marble carving shows women in heavy armor battling one another. The inscription names them as “Amazon” and “Achillia” and mentions that the battle was ruled a tie.

A two-thousand-year-old bronze statuette shows a gladiatrix wearing little armor and brandishing a sica, a short, curved sword, in her left hand. This weapon was often used on an opponent’s bare back. Researchers believe it’s further evidence that women sometimes fought to the death in ancient amphitheaters.

FACT or FAKE?

Nero fiddled while **ROME** burned.

Nero wasn't fiddling while Rome burned.

WHEN THE GREAT FIRE RAGED IN ROME IN 64 CE, THE EMPEROR WAS AT HIS PALACE IN ANTIUM, OUTSIDE THE CITY, AND RUSHED BACK AS SOON AS HE GOT WORD OF THE TRAGEDY.

For a week, the million citizens of ancient Rome watched helplessly as the blaze destroyed 70 percent of the city, leaving half the population homeless. According to the historian Tacitus, Nero coordinated firefighting efforts on the first night. He also opened public buildings and his own gardens as temporary shelter for homeless residents.

So how did the myth begin that Nero fiddled while Rome burned? Because people didn't like him. The emperor was incredibly cruel and had thousands murdered during his reign. Many citizens wanted someone to blame for the tragedy, so they chose him.

The fact that he was a skilled musician only fed into the myth. Nero played a harplike stringed instrument called a *cithara*, and was quite good at it. In fact, he sometimes competed against commoners in music contests.

So is there a chance that Nero fiddled while Rome burned? No. You see, the fiddle wasn't invented until nine hundred years later.

FACT or FAKE?

Slaves built the great **PYRAMIDS** of Egypt.

Despite what you may have seen in movies, the builders of the ancient pyramids of Egypt were not slaves or captured foreigners.

EXCAVATED SKELETONS SHOW THAT THEY WERE EGYPTIAN WORKERS WHO LIVED IN VILLAGES RUN BY SUPERVISORS WHO WORKED FOR THE PHARAOHS. These villages had bakers, butchers, brewers, houses, cemeteries, and even a health clinic.

An estimated twenty to thirty thousand workers built the Great Pyramids at Giza thousands of years ago. Huge limestone blocks, weighing 2.5 to 15 tons, were floated on the Nile River from quarries to the base of the pyramids. Workers polished the stones by hand and then pushed them up ramps to their intended positions.

Archaeologists believe the builders came from poor Egyptian families. They were respected for their work, because those who died during construction were honored by being buried in the tombs near the sacred pyramids of their pharaohs. Those workers would not have been buried so honorably if they were slaves.

SEVEN WONDERS OF THE ANCIENT WORLD

- The Pyramids of Egypt (the only wonder to survive today)
- The Hanging Gardens of Babylon (were in modern-day Iraq)
- The Temple of Artemis at Ephesus (was in modern-day Turkey)
- The Statue of Zeus at Olympia (was in modern-day Greece)
- The Mausoleum of Halicarnassus (was in modern-day Turkey)
- The Colossus of Rhodes (was in modern-day Greece)
- The Lighthouse of Alexandria (was in modern-day Egypt)

Crickets can tell you the **TEMPERATURE** outside.

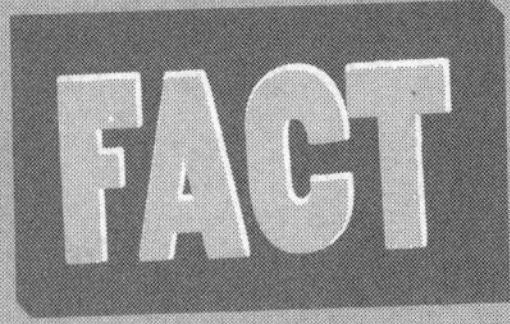

Crickets can indeed tell you the outdoor temperature.

THE FREQUENCY OF CHIRPING VARIES ACCORDING TO TEMPERATURE—THE MORE THEY CHIRP, THE WARMER IT IS. There are two basic formulas you can use to get a rough estimate of the temperature in degrees Fahrenheit: Count the number of chirps in 15 seconds and then add 37. Or count the number of chirps in 13 seconds and then add 40. That should tell you the temperature outside within a couple of degrees. Keep in mind that this works for temperatures between 55 degrees and 95 degrees. Below or above those numbers, the crickets aren't much in the mood for chirping.

Usually, the male crickets are the ones making the noise. They do this by rubbing a sharp edge of one wing against a series of wrinkles on the other wing. The most common reasons why they chirp are to warn off predators and attract female mates.

HOT AND COLD

- Hottest temperature ever recorded on Earth: 134 degrees, Death Valley, CA, July 10, 1913
- Lowest temperature ever recorded on Earth: minus 128.6 degrees, Vostok Station, Antarctica, July 21, 1983
- Lowest temperature in the U.S.: minus 80 degrees, Prospect Creek, AK, January 23, 1971

FACT or FAKE?

A ring around the moon means **RAIN** real soon.

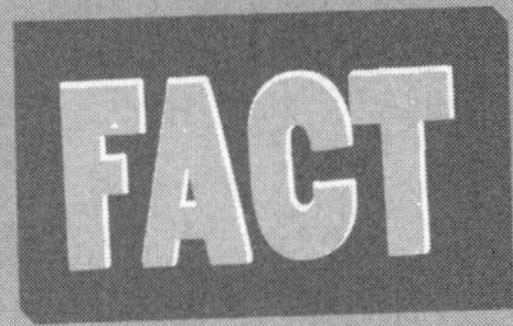

A halo around the moon often is caused by a thin layer of cirrus clouds that move in ahead of an approaching storm system.

(most of the time)

THE RING YOU SOMETIMES SEE AROUND THE MOON IS MORE OF AN OPTICAL ILLUSION, LIKE A RAINBOW. Meteorologists (scientists who study weather) call this a "halo effect," which occurs when bent light rays create a large circle around a bright object.

Moon halos are caused by millions of tiny ice crystals that have gathered at an altitude of twenty thousand feet or more as thin, wispy clouds. It would be hard to notice them if it weren't for the moonlight. Incoming light rays from the moon are bent by these ice crystals to create a large circle. Like a rainbow, this halo sometimes appears in faint shades of color, usually reddish on the inside and bluish on the outside.

RAIN, RAIN, GO AWAY!

- Most rainfall in one minute: 1.5 inches, the Caribbean island of Guadeloupe, November 26, 1970
- Most in one hour: 12 inches, Holt, MO, June 22, 1947
- Most in twenty-four hours: 71.8 inches, the French island of Réunion, January 7–8, 1966
- Most in one year: 1,042 inches, Cherrapunji, India, 1860–1861
- Highest average annual total: 467.4 inches, Mawsynram, India

FACT or FAKE?

HURRICANES are the number-one weather-related killer in the United States.

Excessive heat kills more people than any other weather phenomenon in the United States.

IT CAUSES, ON AVERAGE, MORE THAN FIFTEEN HUNDRED DEATHS EACH YEAR, ACCORDING TO THE NATIONAL OCEANIC AND ATMOSPHERIC ADMINISTRATION (NOAA). In fact, excessive heat claims more lives each year than floods, lightning, tornadoes, and hurricanes combined. From 1936 through 1975, almost twenty thousand people were killed by the effects of heat and solar radiation.

An intense summer heat wave that spread across the nation in 1980 killed more than 1,250 people, and another infamous heat wave in July 1995 took 700 lives in the Chicago area alone. The victims most affected by heat waves are the elderly, small children, people with a chronic disease, residents who live in the heart of large cities, and those who don't have air conditioning or can't afford to run it.

More people die of heat-related causes in cities than in rural areas. That's because buildings and paved surfaces absorb heat during the day and don't cool enough at night.

FACT or FAKE?

The United States has more **TORNADOES** than any other country in the world.

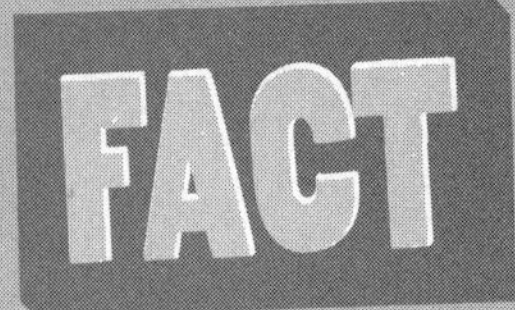

The United States leads the world in twisters, averaging around 1,200 a year.

TORNADOES TOUCH DOWN ON EVERY CONTINENT EXCEPT ANTARCTICA. However, the United States has far more twisters than anywhere else because it has an abundance of flat, low-lying areas, and a climate that triggers the kind of intense thunderstorms that produce tornadoes.

Although every state in the union has been hit by twisters, the area most likely to be hit is called "Tornado Alley," a slice of America's midsection running vertically from Texas through Oklahoma, Kansas, Nebraska, South Dakota, and into North Dakota. Portions of other states such as Colorado, Iowa, Missouri, Arkansas, and Louisiana are also part of this prime breeding ground for twisters.

TEN DEADLIEST TORNADOES IN THE UNITED STATES

- 1925 Tri-State (MO, IL, IN), 695 killed
- 1840 Natchez, MI, 317
- 1896 St. Louis, MO, 255
- 1936 Tupelo, MS, 216
- 1936 Gainesville, GA, 203
- 1947 Woodward, OK, 181
- 2011 Joplin, MO, 158
- 1908 Amite, LA, and Purvis, MS, 143
- 1899 New Richmond, WI, 117
- 1953 Flint, MI, 116

FACT or FAKE?

LIGHTNING never strikes twice in the same place.

There's no reason that lightning wouldn't strike the same place twice.

IF THERE IS A THUNDERSTORM IN A GIVEN AREA, THEN OBJECTS AND PLACES THAT ARE HIGHER THAN THE SURROUNDING AREA OR ARE MADE OF SUBSTANCES THAT ATTRACT LIGHTNING WILL LIKELY BE STRUCK REPEATEDLY. For instance, lightning strikes the Empire State Building in New York City about one hundred times per year.

Lightning is a giant discharge of electricity accompanied by a brilliant flash of light and a loud crack of thunder. The bolt can travel up to sixty thousand miles per second, reach over five miles in length, raise the temperature of the air by as much as fifty thousand degrees Fahrenheit, and contain a hundred million electrical volts.

Obviously, you don't want to be near a lightning bolt. The National Lightning Safety Institute estimates that your house will be hit by a bolt once every two hundred years. The odds of you being struck by lightning during a storm are about one in eight hundred thousand, according to the National Weather Service.

STRIKING OUT

- You can be struck by lightning even when the center of a thunderstorm is ten miles away and the sky is blue directly above you.
- Rubber shoes will not protect you from lightning.
- If you're caught outside during a storm, standing under a tall tree is one of the most dangerous places to find shelter.
- Always avoid being near the highest object, lightning rods, or metal objects such as fences or underground pipes.

FACT or FAKE?
It can RAIN frogs and toads.

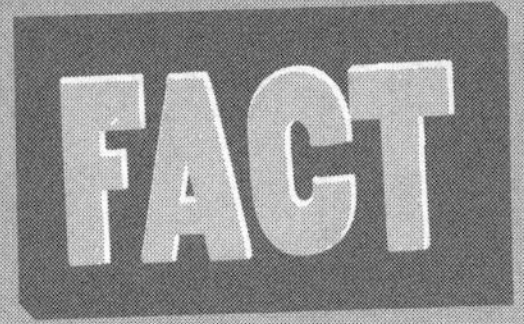

Forget about raining cats and dogs. It sometimes rains frogs and toads—and fish, too.

OKAY, IT DOESN'T HAPPEN OFTEN, BUT THERE HAVE BEEN REPORTS AROUND THE WORLD OF AQUATIC CREATURES RAINING FROM THE SKIES.

Minneapolis was pelted with frogs and toads in July 1901. Frog rains were reported in Japan in 2009 and during a three-day period in 2010 in Hungary. The United Kingdom has seen its share of frog rains and fish rains, too, over the years.

There's an explanation for this freaky weather phenomenon: A small tornado known as a waterspout forms over water, such as a lake or pond, and spins at speeds of up to two hundred miles per hour. It sucks up fish and amphibians that are on or just below the surface and lifts them into the waterspout's swirling low-pressure core, known as a vortex. When the waterspout hits land, it loses some of its energy and slows down. The vortex eventually weakens until it releases whatever it had sucked up, such as frogs and fish. The end result is frog rain or fish rain.

FLOODING causes more damage in the United States than any other severe weather-related event.

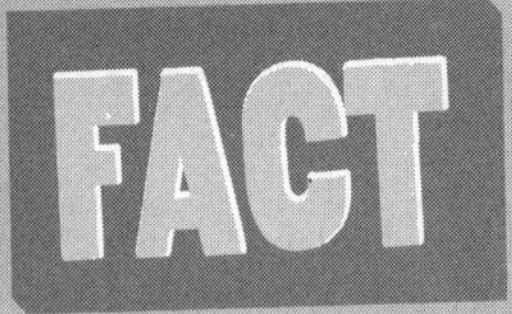

Flooding causes an average of $5 billion in damages a year, according to the National Oceanic and Atmospheric Administration.

DANGEROUS RISING WATER CAN OCCUR IN ANY OF THE FIFTY STATES. The most common cause of flooding is from rain or snowmelt that accumulates faster than the ground can absorb it or rivers can carry it away. No season is safe from flooding. Melting snow combines with rain in early spring. Severe thunderstorms bring heavy downpours in spring and summer. Hurricanes and tropical depressions dump intense rain and create storm surges in the summer and fall. Ice jams or debris jams dam up rivers in the winter. Dams and levees burst.

Three-fourths of all presidential disaster declarations are associated with flooding. Hurricane Katrina in 2005 caused an estimated $48-62 billion in flood-related damages.

RISKY ROADS

Flooded streets can be extremely dangerous. Six inches of fast-moving water can knock you off your feet. Water twenty-four inches deep can carry away most automobiles. Nearly half of all flash-flood deaths occur in automobiles when they are swept downstream. Most of these deaths take place when people drive into flooded roads or low drainage areas.

FACT or FAKE?

RAIN is always colorless.

Rain has fallen in a variety of colors, from reds and yellows to blacks and milky whites.

IT HAPPENS WHEN DUST, SAND, POLLEN, OR POLLUTANTS ARE CARRIED BY THE WIND AND MIX WITH RAIN CLOUDS. Pollens can contribute to yellow rain, and dusts from coal mines have been known to cause black rain. But red rain—sometimes called blood rain—is the most common of colored showers. These rains typically take on the color of weak red juice.

From July 25 to September 23, 2001, reddish rain sporadically fell on the southern Indian state of Kerala. Some people feared that the heavy downpours were somehow mixed with blood. The raindrops actually stained the clothes of people who got caught in the storm or had their garments hanging from the clothesline. In other parts of the state, the rain came down in drops of yellow, green, or black. Scientists eventually determined that the airborne spores from algae growing in local ponds and lakes were responsible for the strange-colored rain.

Red rains have fallen in Europe, too. In most of these cases, the raindrops were colored by dust carried by sandstorms from the Sahara Desert, thousands of miles away in Africa.

FACT or FAKE?

SMOG has killed people sitting in their own homes.

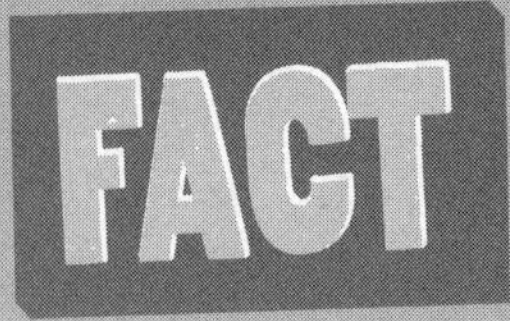

Yes, there is such a thing as killer smog.

SMOG IS THE MIXTURE OF FOG AND SMOKE OR OTHER AIRBORNE POLLUTANTS SUCH AS VEHICLE-EXHAUST FUMES. IT IS A HEALTH HAZARD, AND SOMETIMES A DEADLY ONE.

In 1952, in London, England, a four-day-long polluted smog, known as the Big Smoke, claimed an estimated twelve thousand lives. It was the worst air-pollution event in the history of the United Kingdom. Killer smog struck New York City three times—in 1953 (between 170 and 260 dead), 1962 (200 dead), and 1966 (169 dead).

In Donora, Pennsylvania, in 1948, smog interacted with fumes from the town's zinc and steel plants, leading to the deaths of twenty people and eight hundred animals. The primary cause of death was the zinc-smelting plant's poisonous fluorine gas, which became trapped by the smog. Autopsy results showed that fluorine levels in the victims were in the lethal range, as much as twenty times higher than normal.

BIRTH OF THE EPA

The Donora disaster spurred the adoption of the Air Pollution Control Act of 1955, the first of several federal laws that led to the passage of the historic Clean Air Act of 1970. Later that year, the Environmental Protection Agency (EPA) was created to develop and enforce regulations to protect the public from exposure to hazardous pollutants.

FACT or FAKE?

It can't **THUNDER** during a snowstorm.

There is such a thing as thundersnow.

ALTHOUGH RARE, THUNDER AND LIGHTING CAN OCCUR DURING EXCEPTIONALLY STRONG SNOW SQUALLS, MOST OFTEN IN LATE WINTER OR EARLY SPRING.

For thundersnow to occur, the layer of air closest to the ground has to be moist and warmer than the layers above, but still cold enough to create snow. When these layers become unstable and the temperatures fall below freezing, they can create this little-known weather phenomenon, which usually accompanies a rapid snowfall.

During a January 9, 2011, snowstorm that blanketed Huntsville, Alabama, Mother Nature treated the locals to some thundersnow. One witness described it "as if a wizard was hurling lightning behind a huge white curtain."

Scientists say the best spots for seeing thundersnow are Wolf Creek Pass, Colorado, and the eastern shores of Lake Ontario.

SNOW KIDDING!

Among the greatest snowfall records in the U.S. are:

- In one month: 313 inches, Tamarack, CA, March 1907
- In 24 hours: 76 inches, Silver Lake, CO, Apr. 14–15, 1921
- In one storm: 189 inches, Mt. Shasta Ski Bowl, CA, Feb. 13–19, 1959
- In one season: 1,140 inches, Mount Baker, WA, 1998–1999

EARTH is slowing down.

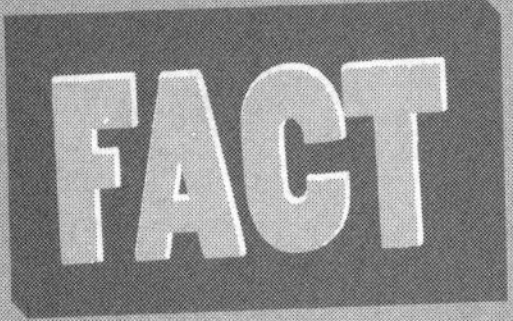

If the day feels like it's dragging, that's because it is—in an extremely small way.

YOU SEE, EARTH IS TAKING LONGER AND LONGER TO COMPLETE ONE FULL TURN, WHICH MAKES UP ONE DAY, TECHNICALLY KNOWN AS A SOLAR DAY.

The rotation of our planet is slowing down because of tidal and gravitational forces between the earth and the moon. Over the span of one hundred years, our day gets about 1.4 milliseconds, or 1.4 thousandths of a second, longer. Okay, that's not much. But if you add up those milliseconds over centuries, it can make a difference.

During the age of the dinosaurs, Earth completed one rotation in about 23 hours. By 1820, a rotation took exactly 24 hours. Since 1820, our day has increased by about 2.5 milliseconds.

Because Earth is slowing down—even though it's ever so slightly—the world's official clocks added an extra "leap" second at midnight, June 30, 2012, to factor in the reduced speed of the planet's rotation.

OUR BIG BLUE BALL

- Seventy percent of Earth's surface is water.
- Earth is made up of 32 percent iron, 30 percent oxygen, 15 percent silicon, 14 percent magnesium, and 9 percent other minerals.
- Because Earth's rotation causes our planet to bulge in the middle, its diameter at the equator measures thirteen miles more than it does from pole to pole.

FACT or FAKE?

The rocket-powered **PLANE** flown by Chuck Yeager in 1947 was the first human-made object to break the sound barrier.

Chuck Yeager's rocket-powered plane was not the first man-made object to break the sound barrier.

WHAT ABOUT THE FIRST LAUNCHED FIRECRACKER OR THE FIRST FIRED BULLET? They're good guesses, but they're wrong. The first object made by man that broke the sound barrier is the whip.

When you snap a whip, it sends a wave down its length. If you are strong enough and use a relatively long whip, you can make the tip of the whip travel faster than the speed of sound, creating a distinctive cracking noise. This cracking is actually the result of a miniature sonic boom.

No one knows when a whip first broke the sound barrier, because it was invented before the dawn of recorded history. In any event, it is likely that whips have been traveling faster than the speed of sound for at least five thousand years.

MACH MADNESS

- On October 14, 1947, test pilot Chuck Yeager became the first person to break the sound barrier in his rocket-powered Bell X-1.
- The actual speed of sound varies depending on the temperature and altitude. At sea level, the speed of sound is around 760 miles per hour.
- A Mach number refers to the measure of air speed, with Mach 1 being the speed of sound. On his first supersonic flight, Yeager flew at 43,000 feet and blasted through the sound barrier at Mach 1.06, or about 700 miles an hour.

FACT or FAKE?

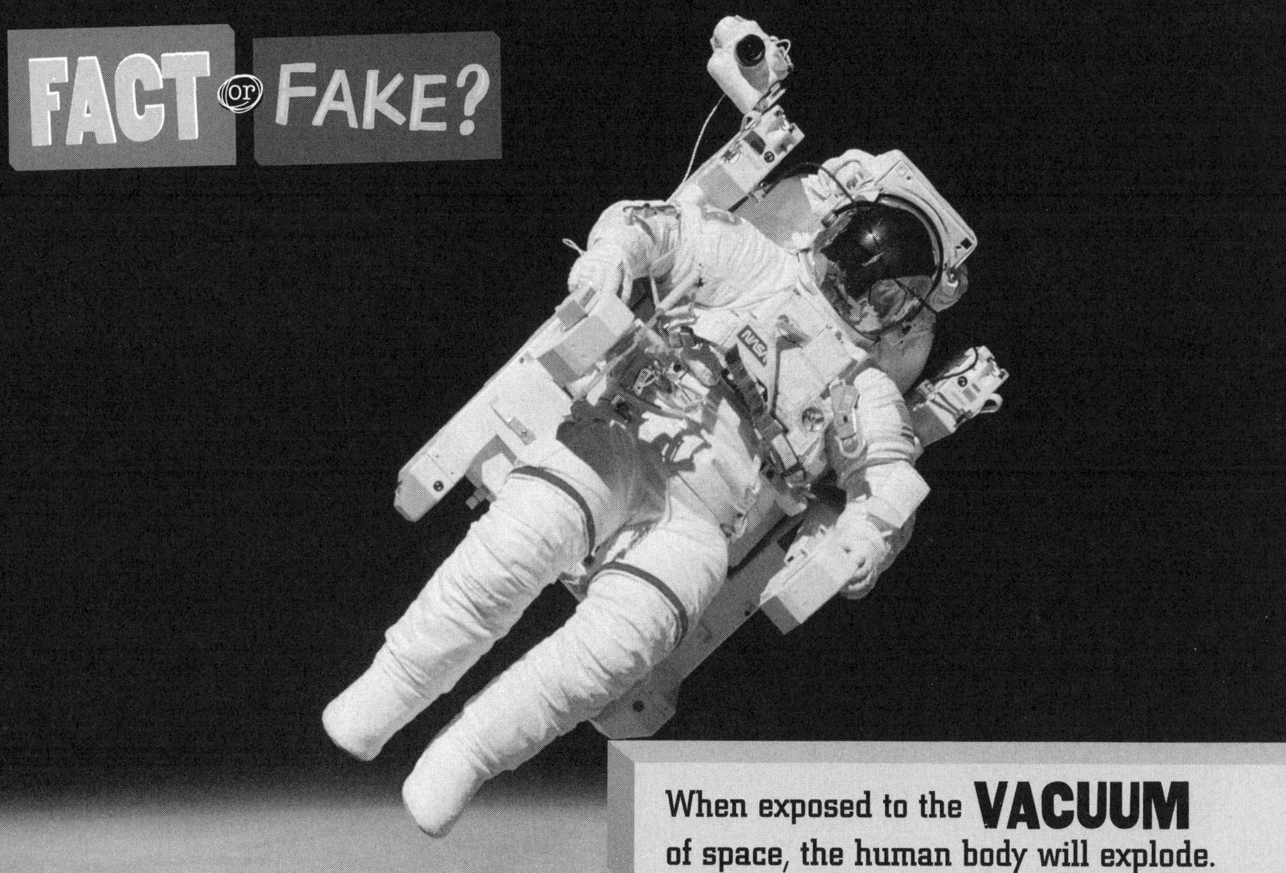

When exposed to the **VACUUM** of space, the human body will explode.

If you are exposed to the vacuum of space for more than a couple of minutes, you will die from asphyxiation—lack of oxygen—but you won't blow up.

ACCORDING TO THE GODDARD SPACE FLIGHT CENTER, IF YOU DON'T TRY TO HOLD YOUR BREATH, EXPOSURE TO SPACE FOR HALF A MINUTE OR SO SHOULDN'T PRODUCE PERMANENT INJURY. Holding your breath for too long will damage your lungs and cause pain to your eardrums, things scuba divers have to watch out for when rising too quickly to the surface.

So if you're exposed in outer space, you have precious little time to get back into a secure spacecraft or spacesuit before you die from a lack of oxygen. If you don't make it, your body won't disintegrate, but it will end up freeze-dried because all the moisture in it will evaporate and the severe cold of space will preserve it.

FACT or FAKE?

If you could put the planet **SATURN** in a gigantic bowl of water, it would float.

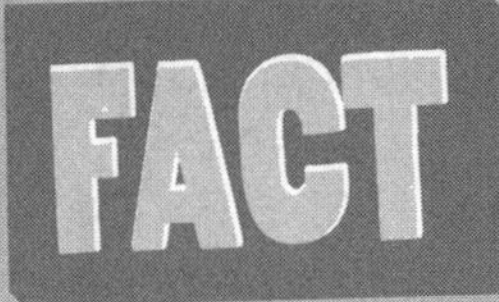

Saturn is a lightweight.

THE SIXTH PLANET FROM THE SUN IS MOST NOTED FOR THE BEAUTIFUL RINGS OF ICE PARTICLES THAT ENCIRCLE IT. Yet even though it's second to Jupiter as the largest planet in our solar system, it's not heavy by planetary standards. In fact, if you could find a big enough bowl of water—one that was many times bigger than Earth—Saturn would actually float.

Despite its size (more than 750 Earths could fit in it), Saturn is made up mostly of gases that are less dense than water. Because it is lighter than water, the planet can float. None of the other planets in our solar system can do this, because they have a higher density and are heavier than water.

OUT OF THIS WORLD

- Venus is our solar system's hottest planet, because its thick atmosphere traps the heat. The surface temperature is between 800 and 900 degrees.
- Uranus is the coldest planet, because its core is cooler than any of the other planets. The temperature can dip to 370 degrees below zero.
- Jupiter has the fastest day in the solar system. It takes slightly less than ten hours for the planet to complete one full rotation.
- In 2006, the International Astronomical Union stripped Pluto of its status as a planet, leaving the solar system with only eight planets instead of nine.

FACT or FAKE?

One side of the **MOON** is always dark.

Many people assume that the dark side of the moon never gets sunlight. But they are wrong. Every part of the moon is illuminated at some time by the sun.

THE MISCONCEPTION IS CAUSED BY THE FACT THAT ONE SIDE OF THE MOON—WHAT SCIENTISTS REFER TO AS THE FAR SIDE—IS NEVER VISIBLE TO US ON EARTH. Here's why: Millions of years ago, as it orbited Earth, the moon spun on its axis at a much faster pace than it does now. However, over time Earth's gravitational influence gradually slowed the moon's rotation to match that of its orbit around Earth—about 29.5 days.

Because the moon's rotational period and its orbital period are virtually identical, we on Earth always see only the same half of the moon—the near side.

Therefore, the far side is never visible to us on Earth. The moon's far side was first photographed by the Soviet Union's unmanned spacecraft Luna 3 in 1959. And guess what? The landscape on the far side is just as rugged, pockmarked, and desolate as the surface on the near side.

FACT or FAKE?

The **MOON** will eventually crash into Earth.

The moon is not going to crash into Earth.

IN FACT, THE MOON IS ACTUALLY DRIFTING AWAY FROM US, BUT AT A VERY *SLOW* RATE OF 3.8 CENTIMETERS A YEAR, OR ABOUT 1.5 INCHES.

The distance from the center of our planet to the center of the moon is nearly 239,000 miles, but that is changing, however sluggishly.

As the moon inches farther away from us, it eventually will have little bearing on our tides. But none of us will be around to see it. Scientists estimate that at the speed the moon is moving away from Earth, it will be another five hundred million years before it loses its influence on our planet.

MAN IN THE MOON

The remains of a scientist are spread on the moon.

Dr. Eugene Shoemaker, who taught Apollo mission astronauts about planetary geology, always dreamed of going into space. But he never made it—at least when he was alive.

Shoemaker died in 1997. Two years later, some of his ashes were carried to the moon aboard the *Lunar Prospector* spacecraft. After the probe carried out its mission of transmitting data about the moon, it was deliberately crashed into the lunar surface, spreading his ashes and fulfilling his final wish.

FACT or FAKE?

It's impossible to **STAND** perfectly still.

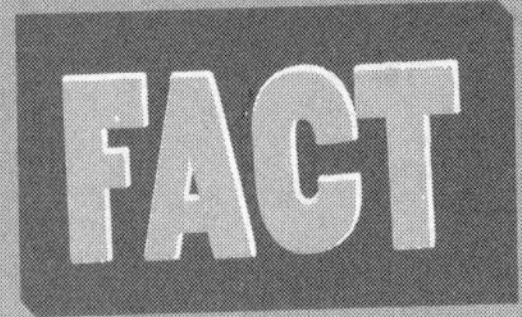

No person or animal, or any object no matter how massive, is ever standing still. We and everything on this planet are in constant motion.

THAT'S BECAUSE EARTH IS SPINNING ON ITS AXIS, MAKING A COMPLETE ROTATION IN 24 HOURS, WHICH ACCOUNTS FOR OUR DAY. (IF YOU WANT TO BE A STICKLER ABOUT IT, A DAY IS REALLY 23 HOURS, 56 MINUTES, AND 4.09053 SECONDS.) If you are standing firmly on the ground on the equator, you are actually moving at almost a thousand miles an hour. If you are standing anywhere in the United States, you're not moving quite so fast, but you're still zipping along at nearly that speed.

We don't notice we're in motion—even if we're lying perfectly still in bed—because Earth's gravity holds us tight to the surface.

But we're all going much faster than 1,000 miles an hour. In addition to spinning on its axis, Earth also revolves around the sun at 67,000 miles per hour. At that speed, you could get from New York to Los Angeles in about three minutes.

But we're moving even more. Our solar system, which includes the sun and its planets, is whirling around the center of our galaxy, the Milky Way, at 490,000 miles per hour. And yes, our galaxy is also rushing headlong into deep space at nearly 600 miles per second, or roughly 2,160,000 miles an hour! Whew!

FACT or FAKE?

The largest living organism in the world is a giant **FUNGUS.**

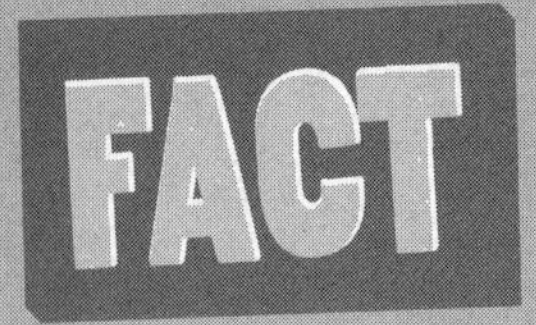

The largest living thing is not a whale or an elephant or any other animal. It's a humungous fungus.

THE HONEY MUSHROOM—AN INVASIVE SPECIES OF FUNGUS—HAS BEEN GROWING IN MALHEUR NATIONAL FOREST IN OREGON FOR CENTURIES AND NOW COVERS A WHOPPING 2,200 ACRES. Scientifically known as the *Armillaria ostoyae*, this monster isn't easy to spot, because most of it spreads underground, out of sight. Occasionally, during the fall season, this specimen will send up golden-colored "honey mushrooms" that give visible evidence of its hulking mass beneath.

From a single microscopic spore, the *Armillaria ostoyae* has been spreading its black shoestring threads throughout the forest for an estimated 2,400 years. That's not a good thing, because the more this giant fungus grows, the more trees it kills. From end to end, this mushroom-like organism is about 3.5 miles wide and three feet thick. It's so huge that it could cover 1,665 football fields.

FACT or FAKE?

Sir Isaac Newton came up with his Universal Law of Gravitation when an **APPLE** fell on his head.

An apple did not hit Sir Isaac Newton on the head.

ACCORDING TO LEGEND, NEWTON WAS SITTING UNDER A TREE WHEN AN APPLE FELL AND BONKED HIM ON HIS HEAD. On the spot, he discovered the Universal Law of Gravitation. But it's a myth—at least the part about getting hit on the noggin.

For a scientist who kept detailed notes, Newton didn't leave any written account that even hinted that such an event happened. However, there are at least two manuscripts from others who claimed that when Newton was an old man, he told them that a fallen apple played a key role in his thinking up the theory of gravity.

William Stukeley, who wrote the first biography about Newton, said that in 1726, a year before the famed British scientist died at the age of eighty-five, the two of them were in Newton's garden in Lincolnshire, England, having tea under an apple tree. According to Stukeley, Newton recalled that in 1666, when he was a twenty-four-year-old Cambridge scholar, he saw an apple fall from a tree, inspiring him to formulate the law of gravitation. The scientist's former assistant, John Conduitt, also wrote that Newton told him the same story.

Whether or not it's true, it doesn't really matter. The story of the falling apple has gone down in history as one of the greatest "Eureka!" moments in science.

FACT or FAKE?

Albert Einstein failed **MATH** in high school.

Einstein was a genius from a young age—including in the field of mathematics.

HE EARNED TOP GRADES IN MATH AND SCIENCE ALL OF HIS LIFE, ALTHOUGH HIS GRADES WERE SOMETIMES AVERAGE IN SEVERAL OTHER SUBJECTS.

It took a while before the world realized that Einstein was brilliant. In 1905, he was working in a Swiss patent office. During his spare time, he produced four papers that upended physics. He showed that light could be particles as well as waves. He proved the existence of atoms and molecules. He created the special theory of relativity, which said that there was no such thing as absolute time or space. And he discovered a special relationship between energy and mass when he penned the most famous equation in all of physics: $E = mc^2$.

During the height of Einstein's popularity, the famous syndicated newspaper feature *Ripley's Believe It or Not!* ran an item under the heading "Greatest living mathematician failed in mathematics!" According to biographer Walter Isaacson, Einstein laughed when he saw the column and said, "I never failed in mathematics. Before I was fifteen I had mastered differential and integral calculus."

And yet the myth persists. A recent Google search of "Einstein failed math" turned up more than 1.6 million references.

FACT or FAKE?

GEOGRAPHY

The **GREAT WALL OF CHINA** is the only man-made structure visible from space.

You can't see the Great Wall of China from outer space.

IN LOW ORBIT (ABOUT ONE HUNDRED MILES UP) AROUND EARTH, ASTRONAUTS HAVE SPOTTED THE 5,500-MILE-LONG BARRIER—BUT AT THAT ALTITUDE THEY'VE ALSO SEEN ROADS AND OTHER MAN-MADE OBJECTS. In fact, there is no distance from Earth at which you can see only the Great Wall and no other structures built by humans.

This myth dates back decades, though no one's sure where it started. A 1932 *Ripley's Believe It or Not!* cartoon helped spread the myth when it claimed that the wall is "the mightiest work of man, the only one that would be visible to the human eye from the moon." People have believed it ever since.

One of the most frequently asked questions to Neil Armstrong, who was the first man to set foot on the moon, was, "Could you see the Great Wall?" In a NASA Johnson Space Center oral history, Armstrong said he saw continents, lakes, and splotches of white on blue. But he could not make out any man-made structures from the moon, which is about 239,000 miles from Earth.

FACT or FAKE?

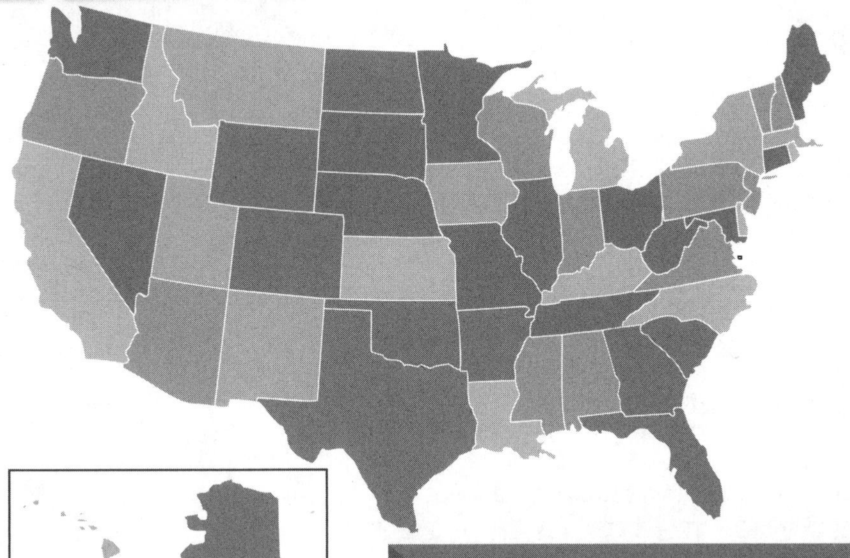

The **UNITED STATES** is really made up of only forty-six states.

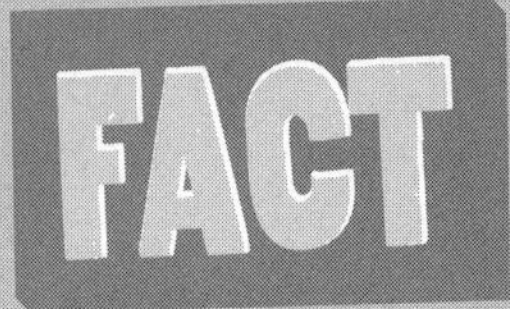

We always talk about our country's fifty states. But technically speaking, our union has only forty-six states. What about the other four? They're commonwealths.

MASSACHUSETTS, PENNSYLVANIA, KENTUCKY, AND VIRGINIA OFFICIALLY USE THE NAME "COMMONWEALTH." So what's the difference between a commonwealth and a state? Nothing, really, because from a constitutional standpoint, they're the same.

The original meaning of commonwealth is a government based on the common consent of the people, not of a king. So when the American colonies declared their independence from Great Britain, the three hotbeds of revolution—Massachusetts, Pennsylvania, and Virginia—wanted to make clear the difference between British rule and a government by the people. The three colonies called themselves commonwealths. In 1792, when Kentucky, which had been a part of Virginia, was formed, it kept the commonwealth status.

NOMBRES BONITOS

States that have names with Spanish origins include:

- Arizona, possibly from *árida zona,* meaning "arid zone"
- Florida, meaning "flowery," because the land was lush with flowers when it was discovered by Ponce de León
- Montana, from *montaña,* meaning "mountain"
- Nevada, meaning "snowy," from *Sierra Nevada,* which is Spanish for "snow-capped range of mountains"

FACT or FAKE?

The smallest country in the world is **VATICAN CITY.**

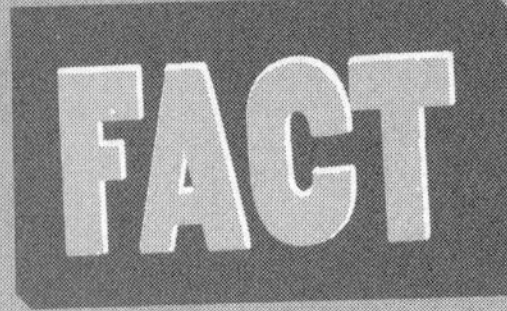

Vatican City is the most itsy-bitsy country on the globe.

IT'S THE SMALLEST INDEPENDENT STATE BY BOTH LAND AREA AND POPULATION. With an area that is only 0.17 square miles, or 108 acres, it's much smaller than the 840-acre Central Park in New York City.

A walled-in sovereign city-state, Vatican City lies in the heart of Rome, Italy, and has a population of slightly more than nine hundred people. It has its own post office and it issues passports. As the home of the Pope and the revered St. Peter's Basilica, Vatican City is the spiritual center and governing body for the world's one billion Roman Catholics.

At 0.77 square miles, the next littlest country is Monaco, which is nestled along the French Riviera on the Mediterranean coast near the city of Nice, France. More than thirty-two thousand people live in this state, which is known for its Monte Carlo casinos and as a playground for the rich and famous.

BIGGEST NATIONS

The world's five largest countries, by area, are:

- Russia 6,592,769 sq. mi.
- Canada 3,851,808 sq. mi.
- United States 3,717,811 sq. mi.
- China 3,705,405 sq. mi.
- Brazil 3,286,487 sq. mi.

FACT or FAKE?

From its base to its summit, Mount Everest is the tallest **MOUNTAIN** in the world.

At its peak of 29,035 feet above sea level, Mount Everest is definitely the highest mountain, but it isn't the tallest.

YOU MIGHT WONDER, *AREN'T "HIGHEST" AND "TALLEST" THE SAME THING?* Not when it comes to geography. Here's why: To determine the tallest mountain, you have to measure it from its base to its tip-top. To calculate the highest mountain, all you have to measure is its height from sea level.

Although Mount Everest wins the distinction of being the highest, it comes in second as the tallest. That honor goes to Hawaii's dormant volcano Mauna Kea. When measured from its underwater base in the Hawaiian Trough to its summit of 13,796 feet above sea level, Mauna Kea stands 33,476 feet tall—which is 4,441 feet taller than Mount Everest.

So the next time you hear someone say that Mount Everest is the tallest mountain in the world, you can sound like a smarty-pants by saying, "No, it's the *highest* but not the *tallest*."

FACT or FAKE?

The needle of a **COMPASS** does not point directly north.

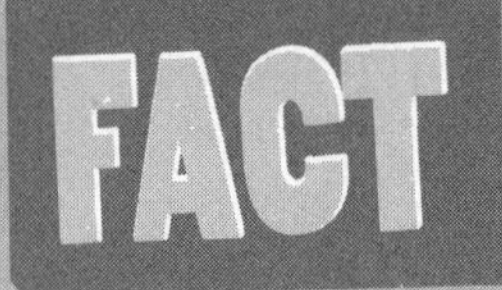

Although a compass is a great tool for navigation, it doesn't necessarily point exactly north. It points either a little to the east or a little to the west.

THAT'S BECAUSE EARTH HAS TWO NORTH POLES. There's the *geographic* North Pole, or "true north," at the top of our planet's axis (an imaginary straight line around which the earth spins). The other is the *magnetic* North Pole, which is where compass needles point. (There are geographic and magnetic South Poles, too.)

The needle on a compass is magnetized and is suspended so it can move freely and point to the magnetic north. The magnetic North and South Poles are the ends of a large magnetic field that surrounds Earth. Because this magnetic field continues to shift over time, the magnetic North Pole lies about one thousand miles south of true north in Canada. Over the last century, it has moved more than 620 miles toward Siberia.

The difference between true north and magnetic north is called declination. Usually it's not enough to make a difference to the average hiker who is looking for a general direction. But those who need pinpoint accuracy must use a declination chart, which can tell them how many degrees they need to adjust on their compass.

When you go hiking, make sure to bring your compass!

FACT or FAKE?
TOURISTS are discouraged from traveling to La Paz, Bolivia, if they have heart or lung conditions.

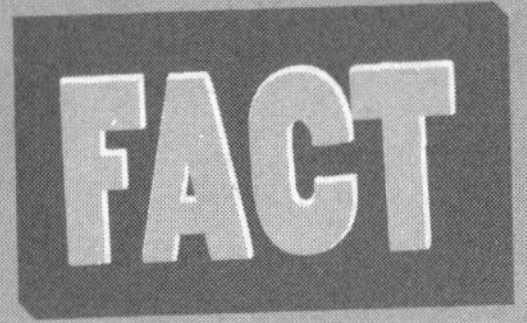

Tourists with medical conditions would be wise to travel someplace other than La Paz, Bolivia.

AT 11,900 FEET ABOVE SEA LEVEL—MORE THAN TWO MILES HIGH—LA PAZ IS THE HIGHEST BIG CITY IN THE WORLD. At that height, many healthy travelers get altitude sickness, sometimes called acute mountain sickness. It's caused by a combination of reduced air pressure and lower oxygen levels at high altitudes.

Symptoms range from mild to life-threatening and can affect the nervous system, lungs, muscles, and heart. That's why travelers with heart or lung conditions are advised against going to La Paz. In most cases, the symptoms for healthy tourists include shortness of breath, confusion, dizziness or light-headedness, fatigue, headache, loss of appetite, and nausea.

Tourists to La Paz ward off altitude sickness by drinking a hot cup of coca leaf tea when they arrive. It's so effective that many airport taxi drivers keep a thermos in their car and offer a tiny cup of coca tea to passengers on the way to their hotel. The coca leaf calms the stomach. Altitude sickness is such a common problem in La Paz that even the larger hotels have oxygen tanks on hand for their guests.

FACT or FAKE?

The Sahara is the world's biggest **DESERT.**

Antarctica—the icy continent at the southernmost part of the world—is the largest desert on Earth.

HOW CAN THAT BE? Well, deserts don't have to be hot; they just have to be arid, which means they get little, if any, rainfall. Antarctica is a cold desert covered almost entirely by ice that averages at least one mile in thickness. As the coldest, driest, and windiest place on our planet, Antarctica's inland has never seen any precipitation at all.

The Sahara isn't even the second biggest desert. That honor goes to the Arctic, which is also considered a desert because its basin receives so little precipitation: less than ten inches a year.

Although the Sahara, which spreads across most of northern Africa, is the planet's third largest desert, it is by far the biggest hot desert.

WORLD'S 5 LARGEST DESERTS

RANK	NAME	AREA/SQ MILES	LOCATION
1	Antarctic Desert	5,339,573	Antarctica
2	Arctic	5,300,000	Alaska, Canada, Finland, Greenland, Iceland, Norway, Russia, and Sweden
3	Sahara	3,320,000+	Algeria, Chad, Egypt, Eritrea, Libya, Mali, Mauritania, Morocco, Niger, Sudan, Tunisia, and Western Sahara
4	Arabian Desert	900,000	Saudi Arabia, Jordan, Iraq, Kuwait, Qatar, United Arab Emirates, Oman, and Yemen
5	Gobi Desert	500,000	Mongolia and China

FACT or FAKE?

ENGLISH is the most widely spoken language in the world.

The world's most widely spoken language is Mandarin, which is used in mainland China, Hong Kong, Macao, Singapore, and Taiwan.

WITH ITS VARIOUS DIALECTS, MANDARIN IS SPOKEN AS A FIRST OR SECOND LANGUAGE BY 1.21 BILLION PEOPLE, ACCORDING TO *ETHNOLOGUE*, AN ENCYCLOPEDIA THAT CATALOGUES THE WORLD'S 6,909 KNOWN LANGUAGES.

Coming in second place is Spanish, spoken by 329 million people. It is the official language of twenty-one countries.

The next most widely spoken language is English, used by 328 million people. Rounding out the top five are Arabic, the official language of twenty-six countries, spoken by 221 million; and Hindi (or Hindustani), which is the official language of India, spoken by 182 million as a first language.

WORDY FACTS

- Language with the most words: English; about 250,000 distinct words
- Language with the fewest words: Taki Taki (also called Sranan); only 340 words; an English-based Creole spoken by 120,000 people in the South American country of Suriname
- Language with the shortest alphabet: Rotokas; 12 letters; an East Papuan language spoken by 4,300 people in the Bougainville Province of Papua New Guinea
- Oldest written languages still in existence: Chinese and Greek; since about 1500 BC

FACT or FAKE?

The world produces enough **FOOD** to feed everyone on the planet.

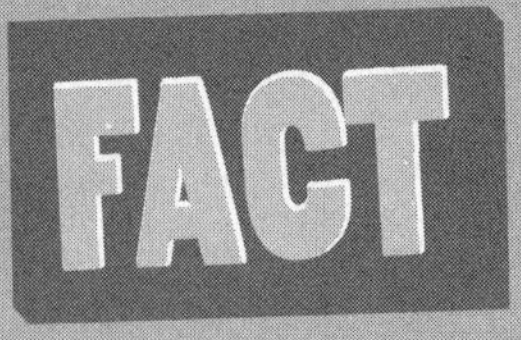

There is enough food in the world today for every one of the planet's seven billion people to have the nourishment necessary for a healthy and productive life.

WORLD AGRICULTURE PRODUCES 17 PERCENT MORE CALORIES PER PERSON TODAY THAN IT DID THIRTY YEARS AGO, DESPITE A 70 PERCENT POPULATION INCREASE DURING THAT TIME. This is enough food to provide every person in the world with at least 2,700 calories per day, according to the United Nations Food and Agriculture Organization.

Sadly, an estimated 925 million men, women, and children—that's 13.1 percent, or almost one in seven people—go hungry every day. Of these chronically hungry people, more than half live in Asia and the Pacific and about 25 percent live in Sub-Saharan Africa (African countries south of the Sahara Desert). An estimated thirty thousand people die each day from malnutrition and hunger.

With all this food on the planet, why is there so much hunger? Poverty, war, drought, and tyranny, along with inefficient distribution of food, are among the main reasons.

FOOD FOR THOUGHT

- More than 93 thousand tons of food is wasted every day in the United States; that totals more than 34 million tons a year.
- Enough food is thrown away every day to fill a pro football stadium.
- A 15 percent reduction in food waste would save enough food to feed 25 million people.

FACT or FAKE?

Throughout recorded history, **NIAGARA FALLS** has never stopped flowing.

For more than twelve thousand years, the mighty falls had always roared—until an ice dam silenced it for two days in March 1848.

GALE-FORCE WINDS HAD PUSHED HUGE CHUNKS OF ICE ON LAKE ERIE UNTIL THEY BLOCKED THE HEAD OF THE NIAGARA RIVER, CAUSING THE FALLS BETWEEN NEW YORK AND ONTARIO TO STOP. When people woke up on March 30, 1848, they were shocked. Some thought the world was coming to an end and packed into their churches. Thousands of others riskily strolled on the dry river bottom, picking up souvenirs and artifacts. People on horseback and horse-drawn buggies paraded up and down the empty river along with U.S. Army cavalry soldiers. Mills and factories shut down because their waterwheels had stopped.

But on the night of March 31, the winds shifted and the air grew warmer, causing the ice pack to break up. And once again, Niagara Falls was flowing.

In 1969, the U.S. Army Corps of Engineers turned off the American side of Niagara Falls by building a temporary dam that diverted the flow to the Canadian Horseshoe Falls. The corps was looking for a way to remove the rocks that had piled up at the base of the American Falls. But after examining the dry falls, the engineers decided it wouldn't be practical, so they turned the river back on.

FACT or FAKE?

ALASKA is the United States's most northern, eastern, and western state.

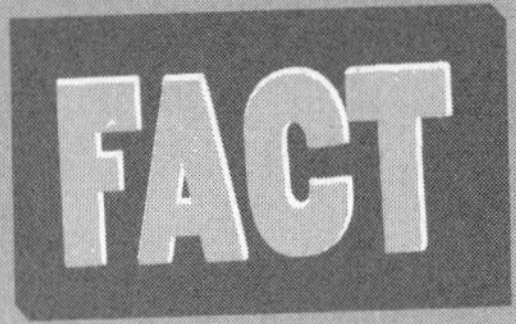

It makes sense that Alaska would be the most northern state in the union. But it's also the most eastern *and* western state.

HOW CAN THAT BE? It has to do with Alaska's Aleutian chain—the string of sixty-nine small islands that extends twelve hundred miles west from the state in the northern Pacific Ocean. By longitude, Alaska's uninhabited Amatignak Island is at the westernmost point of our country. But if you keep traveling west to the very end of the Aleutian chain, you will cross over the 180th meridian, the boundary between the Eastern Hemisphere and the Western Hemisphere. The last of Alaska's islands is the uninhabited Semisopochnoi Island, which sits at 179 degrees, 46 minutes east, making it America's *easternmost* geographic point. Not surprisingly, Alaska also lays claim to having the most extreme northern point in the United States—a headland on the Arctic coast called Point Barrow, where the water is frozen about ten months out of the year.

And where is America's southernmost point? It's not off the Florida coast. In fact, it's way on the other side of the nation—Ka Lae, the southern tip of the big island of Hawaii. Ka Lae, which in Hawaiian means "the point," is registered as a National Historic Landmark District under the name South Point Complex.

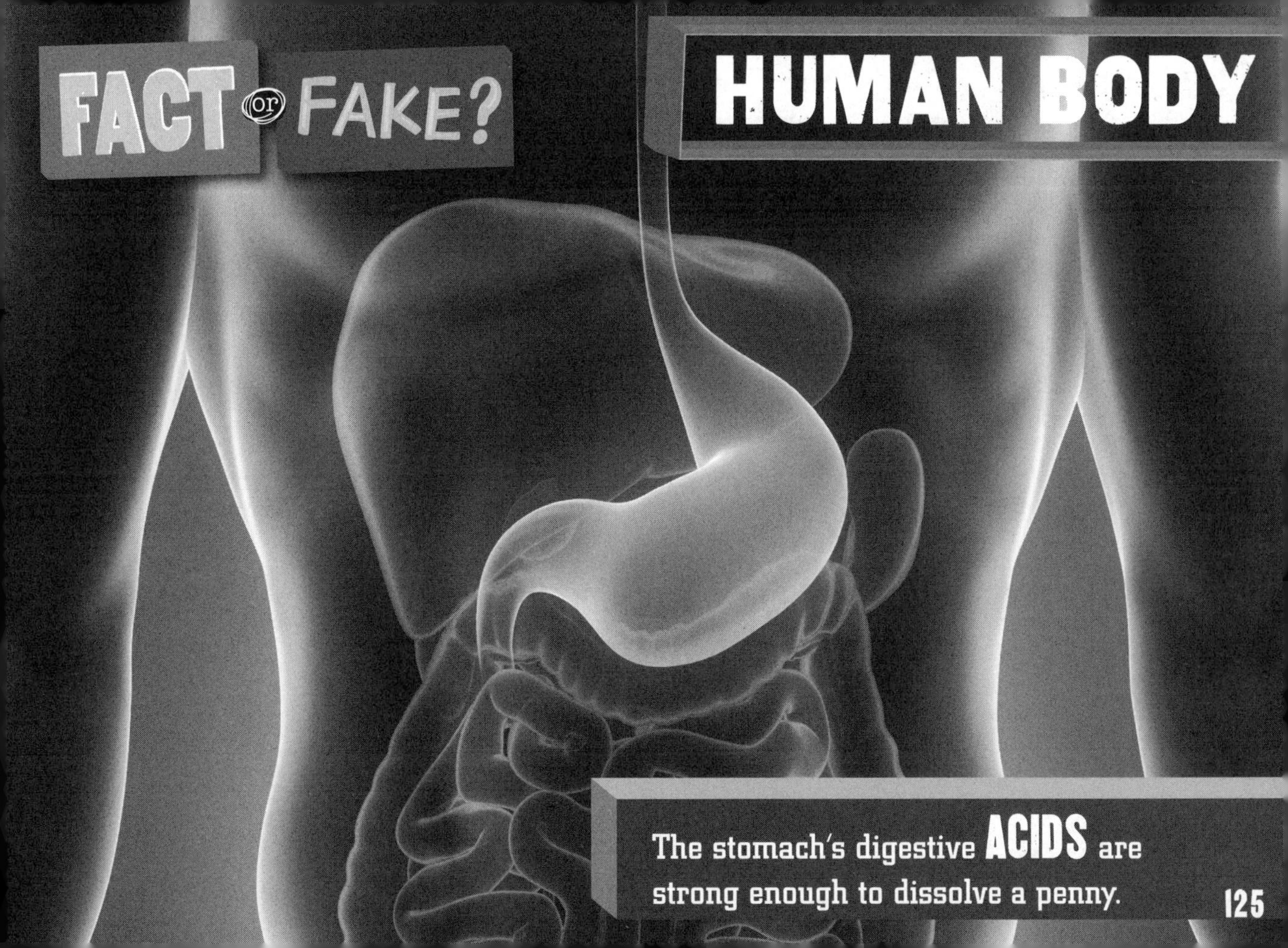

FACT or FAKE?

HUMAN BODY

The stomach's digestive **ACIDS** are strong enough to dissolve a penny.

Your stomach contains a powerful gastric juice called hydrochloric acid that is strong enough to dissolve a penny. However, swallowing a penny would be very harmful to your stomach, so don't try this at home!

THE ACID IS SO CONCENTRATED THAT IF YOU WERE TO PUT A DROP OF IT ON A PIECE OF WOOD, IT WOULD EAT RIGHT THROUGH IT.

About the size of a melon, the stomach is an organ that prepares swallowed food for digestion in the small intestine. Every three seconds, the stomach squirts about a teaspoon of food into the small intestine, so that your meal is usually gone from your stomach within three to five hours. The stomach can hold about a quart of food at a time.

Before food leaves the stomach, it gets broken down into ever-smaller pieces until it forms a slurry (a mixture of liquids and solids). This process is aided by two main gastric juices—hydrochloric acid, which can destroy harmful microorganisms in food, and the protein-splitting enzyme pepsin.

Because stomach acid is strong enough to dissolve a coin, you might wonder why the stomach doesn't destroy itself. The stomach wall, or lining, has a protective layer of mucus-producing cells that deflect acid attack. These cells renew so quickly—every three days—that the acids don't have time to dissolve the lining.

FACT or FAKE?

The **BRAIN** is the body's biggest organ.

Your body's biggest organ isn't your brain, it's your skin.

THE SKIN ACCOUNTS FOR 12 TO 15 PERCENT OF YOUR BODY WEIGHT. In an adult man, skin covers about twenty square feet, which is slightly more than the area of two folding card tables.

Your skin protects the other organs (such as your heart and lungs), bones, muscles, and tissue from harmful bacteria and disease; keeps water in the body; lets you feel and react to heat and cold; and helps regulate your body temperature.

The outer layer of your skin is the epidermis, which is thickest on the palms of your hands and soles of your feet. Beneath the epidermis is the dermis, which consists of connective tissue, and cushions the body from stress and strain. It contains hair follicles, sweat glands, other glands, blood vessels, and the nerve endings that provide the sense of touch.

SKIN DEEP

The average adult human being has about three hundred million skin cells. Because the skin is constantly renewing itself, humans shed about six hundred thousand microscopic particles of skin every hour. That adds up to about 1.5 pounds a year. By the time you are seventy years old, you would have lost 105 pounds of skin!

FACT or FAKE?
You SHRINK every day.

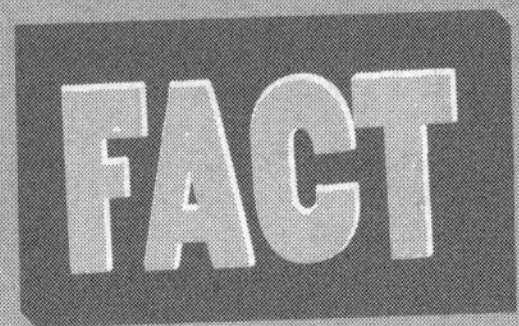

You're just a tad smaller at the end of the day than you were when you first woke up.

HERE'S WHY: YOU HAVE TWENTY-THREE JELLYLIKE CARTILAGE DISKS THAT ACT AS SHOCK ABSORBERS BETWEEN THE SPINAL VERTEBRAE (BONES IN YOUR SPINAL COLUMN). These disks contain as much as 88 percent fluid. As the day goes on, the fluid in these disks are squeezed like sponges by the force of gravity when you stand, walk, or sit.

Not to worry, though. When you sleep, your body recovers and your disks reabsorb fluid. You can grow by more than a half inch during the night, so by morning you're back to your former height or possibly a wee bit taller, depending on your age. But, remember, by bedtime you would have shrunk again.

OH, GROW UP!

The average boy grows fastest between the ages of fourteen and fifteen, while the average girl grows fastest between twelve and thirteen. While she ends her growth spurt at eighteen, he needs another two years before he stops growing.

FACT or FAKE?

You use only 10 percent of your **BRAIN.**

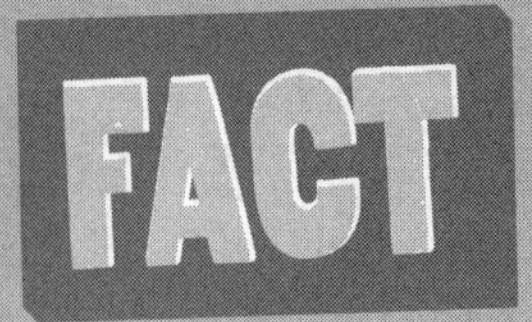

You'd better be using more than 10 percent of your brain, or you won't be functioning.

THE TRUTH IS THAT 100 PERCENT OF YOUR BRAIN IS FULLY INVOLVED ALL THE TIME, EVEN WHEN YOU'RE SLEEPING. Our brains are divided into many different regions that serve different functions. These regions work together to create the complex web of sensation, experience, and knowledge that we all enjoy.

Medical imaging technologies that measure activity in people's brains have enabled scientists to prove that every region of the brain is constantly active at all hours of the day and night.

So the next time an adult tells you to use your brain, you can respond, "I am, all the time!"

FACT or FAKE?

HUMANS don't have any blue blood.

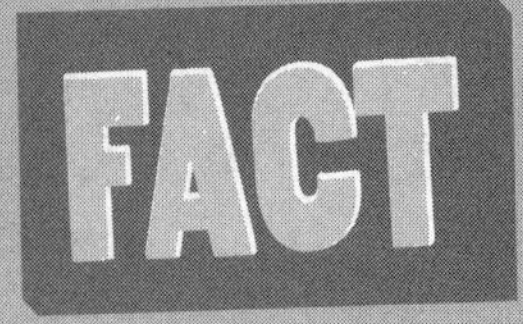

Blue blood does not run in your veins.

YES, THE VEINS IN YOUR ARM LOOK BLUE, BUT THAT'S BECAUSE OF THE WAY LIGHT PASSES THROUGH YOUR SKIN. Your blood is never blue. The blood that flows in your veins (thin tubes that carry blood to the heart) is dark red, while the blood that flows through your arteries (thick, elastic tubes that carry blood from the heart) is bright red.

Your veins look blue because you are looking at them through your skin. The proteins in skin scatter light and make the dark red blood in the veins look bluish when seen against flesh. It doesn't matter what your blood type is—A, B, AB, or O. Blood is red because it is carrying oxygen, which is one of its primary purposes.

BLOOD FACTS

- Seven percent of your body weight is made up of blood.
- Blood is 50 percent water.
- A healthy kidney filters fifty gallons of blood every day.
- The body replaces half of all its red blood cells every week.
- Forty-five percent of all people in the U.S. have Type O (positive or negative) blood.

FACT or FAKE?

You lose most of your body heat through your **HEAD.**

In cold weather, you will lose heat through whatever area of your body isn't covered.

HEAT ESCAPES FROM ANY EXPOSED AREA, SO PUTTING ON A HAT IS NO MORE IMPORTANT THAN SLIPPING GLOVES ON YOUR HANDS.

Your head is only about 10 percent of your body surface area. If the myth were true, your head would have to lose about forty times more heat per square inch than the rest of your body. Studies have proven that a person doesn't lose heat significantly faster through the scalp than through any other portion of the body with the same surface area.

The myth came from a flawed conclusion of a military experiment in the 1950s. Volunteers were dressed in Arctic survival suits and exposed to bitterly cold conditions. Because the only part of their bodies left uncovered were their heads, that's where most of their heat was lost.

The bottom line is: In the wintertime, cover up!

FACT or FAKE?

A pound or two of **BACTERIA** live on or in you.

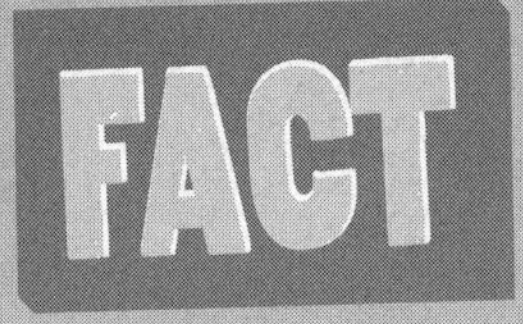

This might sound gross, but up to 3 percent of your body weight is made up of bacteria, fungi, and other microbes.

BEFORE YOU SAY "YUCK!" KEEP IN MIND THAT MANY OF THESE TINY ORGANISMS ARE HELPFUL.

The average adult has between two and five pounds of live bacteria inside the body. The largest concentration of bacteria is found in the intestines. Some of the body's bacteria are harmful and some are helpful.

The bad bacteria get most of the press because of their potential for creating infections and killer diseases like cholera, typhoid, and scarlet fever. That's why Mom is always telling you to wash your hands often and scrub your skin when you take a shower.

However, researchers have discovered that each person carries trillions of good bacteria that live in or on the body. The good bacteria are essential for human life because they help digest food, synthesize certain vitamins, and form a barricade against disease-causing germs.

You have tens of thousands of miles of **BLOOD VESSELS** in your body.

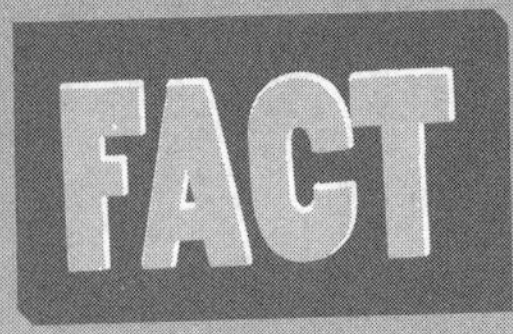

The average adult has about sixty-two thousand miles of blood vessels in his or her body. If laid end-to-end, those vessels would circle Earth more than twice.

BLOOD VESSELS ARE TUBES THAT MAKE UP AN INTRICATE AND COMPLEX SYSTEM THAT CARRIES BLOOD THROUGHOUT THE BODY. Along with the heart and lungs, these vessels make up the circulatory system and ensure healthy body function. When you breathe in and out, blood flows through the vessels to the lungs, dropping off carbon dioxide and picking up oxygen. A similar process takes place when the blood drops off oxygen and nutrients and then returns to the heart.

Your body also has capillaries, which are the smallest blood vessels. They connect arteries and veins and carry blood to and from the trillions of cells in your body.

CATCHING YOUR BREATH

- The lungs of an average person expand and contract from twenty to twenty-five thousand times a day.
- Combined, these twin organs breathe in about 2,100 to 2,400 gallons of air daily.
- An average person takes about fourteen to sixteen breaths per minute, and four to five times that number during exercise.
- There are about six hundred million tiny air sacs, called *alveoli,* in the lungs—enough in just one lung to cover the area of a tennis court if spread out.

An adult has about sixty more **BONES** than a newborn.

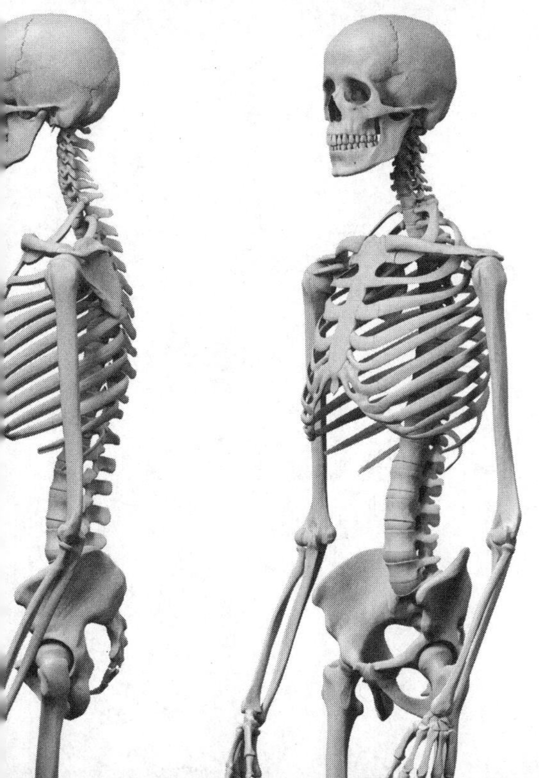

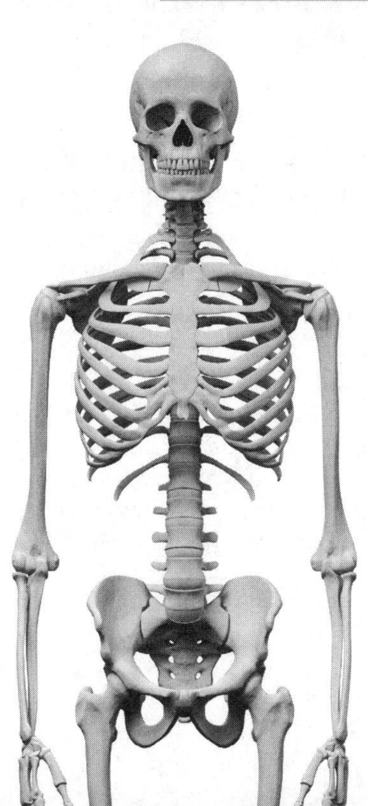

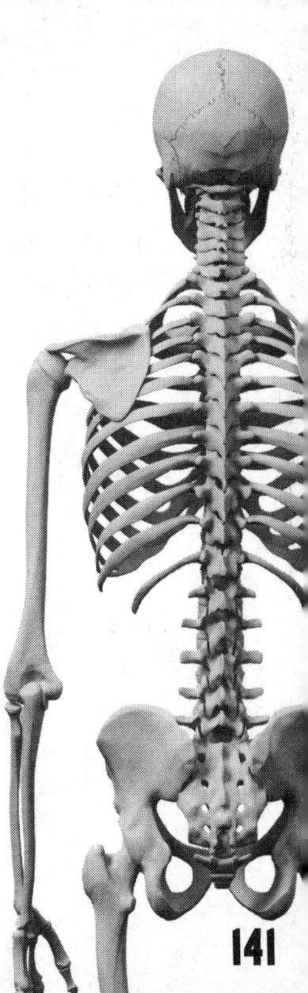

A newborn has about 270 bones, compared to an adult, who has only 206 bones.

A BABY IS BORN WITH CARTILAGE—STRONG, FLEXIBLE, BONELIKE TISSUE—BETWEEN SOME BONES, MOSTLY IN THE SKULL AND SPINE. This gives babies a more flexible body structure and allows faster growth. Because cartilage is slightly softer and more elastic than regular bones, it tends to bend rather than break if the baby should fall.

Throughout childhood, most of this cartilage, especially in the skull and spine, fuses together and becomes hard bones. This process reduces the number of bones in the body over time. Throughout the teenage years, the skeleton continues to get larger and the bones keep getting harder. By your early twenties, your body will end up with 206 fully mature, hardened bones.

So even though you have considerably fewer bones in your body than you had at birth, you nevertheless have a bigger, stronger skeleton.

TAKE A BREAK

Nearly seven million people a year suffer a broken bone. The three most common fractures:

- Collarbone (also known as the clavicle)—the bone most often broken among children
- Arm—accounting for half of all fractures among adults, and second most common among children
- Wrist—accounting for one in every six fractures treated in the emergency room

FACT or FAKE?

Your **FUNNY BONE** is the most sensitive bone in your body.

Your "funny bone" is not a bone at all.

IT'S A LARGE NERVE CALLED THE *ULNAR NERVE,* WHICH RUNS UNDER A BUMP OF BONE ON THE INSIDE PART OF YOUR ELBOW. This nerve controls certain movements in your hand, especially the fourth and fifth fingers.

Because it is the body's largest nerve that isn't protected by either bone or muscle, it is quite sensitive to any kind of impact. That's why you feel a sharp tingling, prickly pain, or weird numbness whenever you accidentally bang your elbow.

So why is it called the "funny bone" when in fact it's a nerve? There are two theories. One is that it is a play on words. The ulnar nerve runs along the humerus, the long bone that starts at your elbow and goes up to your shoulder. *Humerus* sounds like the word *humorous*, which is another word for "funny." The other theory is that its name comes from the strange or funny feeling you get when you smack your elbow.

About the only thing humorous about your funny bone is that it's the only "bone" in your whole body that you can't break!

FACT or FAKE?

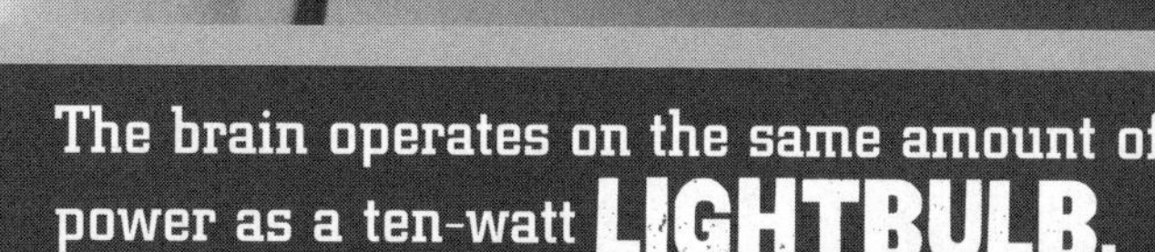

The brain operates on the same amount of power as a ten-watt **LIGHTBULB.**

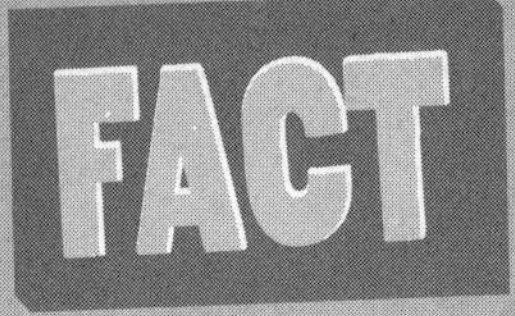

Your brain generates as much energy as a small lightbulb, even when you're sleeping.

YOU'VE PROBABLY SEEN A CARTOON IMAGE OF A LIGHTBULB OVER SOMEONE'S HEAD WHEN A GREAT THOUGHT OCCURS TO HIM OR HER. Well, there's some truth to that. In fact, the brain is much more active at night than during the day. Logically, you would think that all the things you do every day such as reading and answering quizzes and playing games would take a lot more brainpower than lying in bed. It turns out that the opposite is true. Scientists don't yet know why this is, but you can thank the hard work of your brain while you sleep for all those pleasant dreams.

By the way, studies indicate that the higher your IQ, the more you dream. If you can't remember what you dreamed last night, that doesn't mean you're dumb. Most of us find it difficult to recall our dreams, basically because they're so brief. That nightmare might seem like it went on for hours, but the average length of most dreams is only a few seconds, which is hardly enough time to leave an impression in your memory bank.

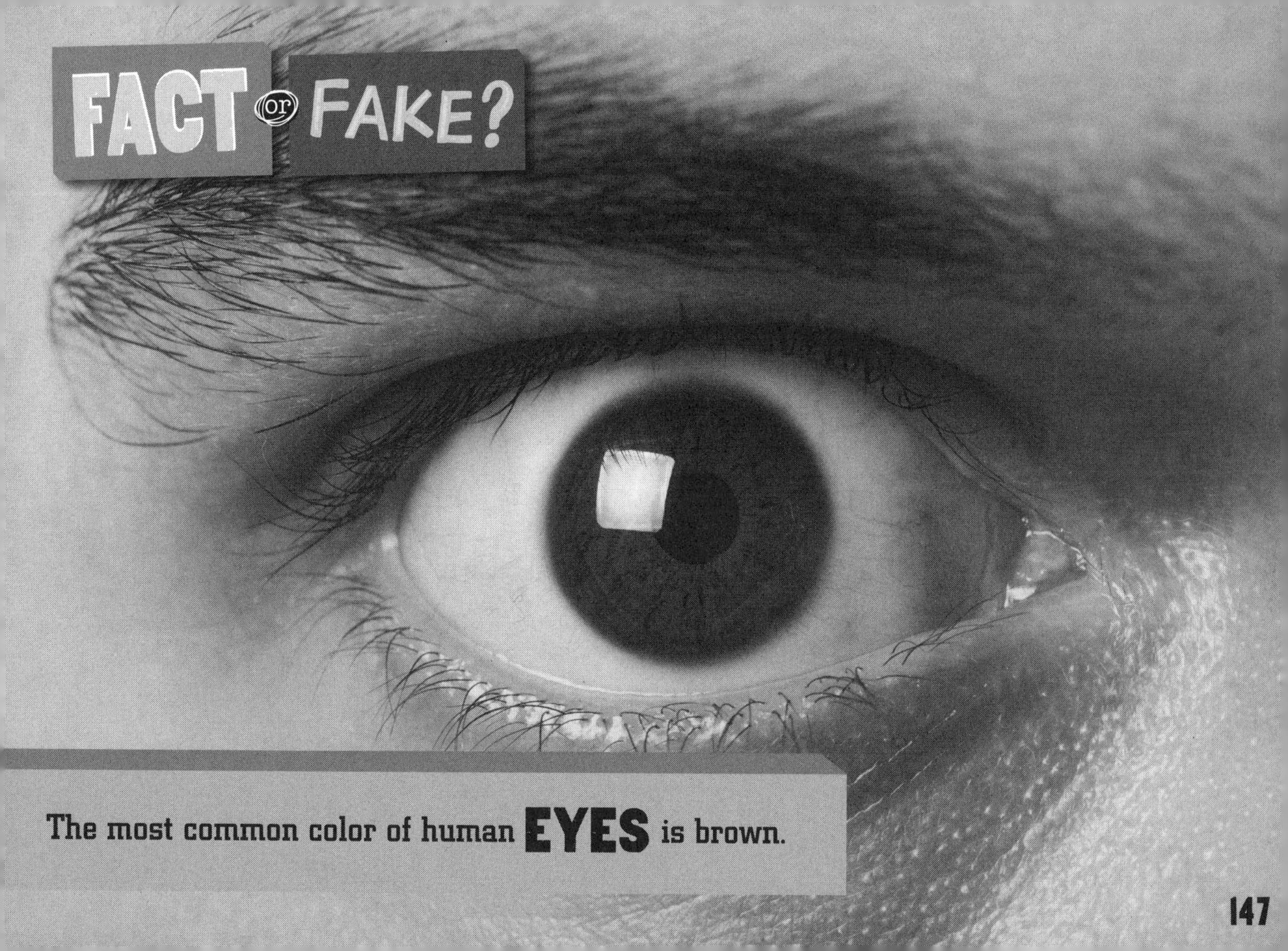

FACT or FAKE?

The most common color of human **EYES** is brown.

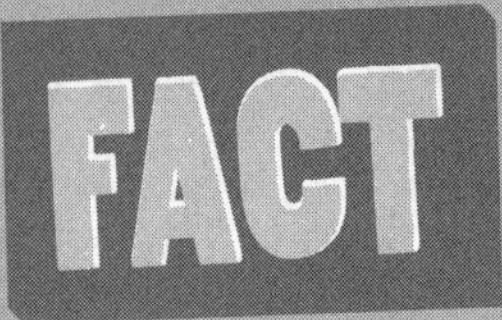

More people throughout the world have brown eyes than any other color.

AND IT'S A COLOR THAT'S COMMON FOR ALL RACES AND IN ALL PARTS OF THE WORLD.

The colored part of the eye is called the iris. Your genes determine its color by the amount and distribution of the pigment melanin, which is usually dark brown. A brown iris contains more melanin than any other color.

Less common basic eye colors include blue (often found among people of European descent with lower levels of melanin), hazel (a combination of green and brown, also among those of European descent), gray (a mix of blue and other colors), and green (typically seen in people of Nordic origin). Green is the rarest color, with only one to two percent of the world's population born with green eyes.

HAIR TODAY, GONE TOMORROW

Black is the most common natural hair color in the world. Because black is so overwhelmingly dominant among people of Asian, Latin, and African descent, it's the natural hair color for an estimated 64 percent of the world's population. Other natural hair colors in order of frequency: brown, auburn, chestnut, gray, white, blond, and red.

FACT or FAKE?
FOOD
CHICKEN SOUP will help you feel better when you have a cold.

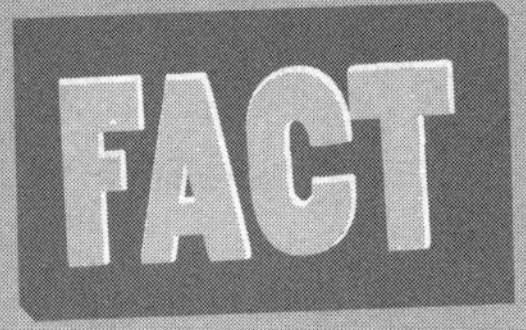

The veggies and hot broth in chicken soup have a positive effect in easing cold symptoms.

ACCORDING TO THE MAYO CLINIC, CHICKEN SOUP HELPS RELIEVE COLD AND FLU SYMPTOMS BY ACTING AS AN ANTI-INFLAMMATORY, BY HELPING RELIEVE CONGESTION, AND BY LIMITING THE AMOUNT OF TIME VIRUSES ARE IN CONTACT WITH THE NOSE LINING.

In 1978, researchers at Mount Sinai Medical Center in Miami Beach, Florida, conducted a study on flu patients using hot water, cold water, and hot chicken soup. The soup proved the most effective liquid in clearing up the nasal passages. A United Kingdom study found that chicken soup can have the same positive effect as taking an over-the-counter cold remedy.

As early as the twelfth century, the rabbi and physician Maimonides wrote that "soup made from an old chicken is of benefit against chronic fevers" and that it "also aids the cough." Soup made with ingredients that make eyes water and noses run—such as garlic, hot peppers, wasabi, and horseradish—is more effective than soup made from blander ingredients.

Scientists say that an amino acid found in chicken is chemically similar to a drug prescribed for bronchitis and other respiratory infections.

FACT or FAKE?

CHOCOLATE causes acne.

Just because you have some zits on your face, it's no reason to blame chocolate.

BACTERIA, STRESS, AND HORMONES ARE THE MOST COMMON CAUSES OF ACNE, ALTHOUGH EATING LARGE AMOUNTS OF CHOCOLATE COULD MAKE YOUR SKIN PROBLEM WORSE.

Studies by the American Academy of Dermatology and the National Institute of Arthritis and Musculoskeletal and Skin Disease have found no connection between chocolate and acne. Although chocolate by itself won't make you break out, a high-sugar, high-fat diet can increase your chances of getting zits.

Eat a balanced diet that includes foods rich in antioxidants, such as green tea, blueberries, and pomegranate; fresh fruits and vegetables; foods high in vitamin A and beta-carotene such as carrots, sweet potatoes, cantaloupe, apricots, kale, and spinach. Avoid eating greasy, fatty, and junk foods.

If you need a chocolate fix, eat dark chocolate—but not too much. Avoid milk chocolate or white chocolate because they have more dairy, sugar, and other additives than dark chocolate. They also can trigger hormonal changes that can cause inflammation, especially for acne-prone people.

THE SKINNY ON SKIN CARE

The best way to avoid, or at least limit, acne:

- Gently wash your face once or twice a day in warm, not hot, water with a moisturizing cleansing bar or facial cleanser containing benzoyl peroxide or salicylic acid.
- Avoid touching your face to prevent the spread of bacteria.
- Stay out of the sun.
- Exercise daily.

FACT or FAKE?

An **APPLE** a day keeps the doctor away.

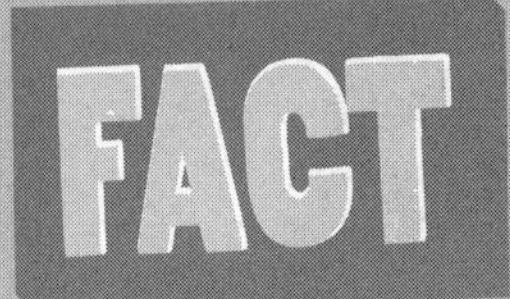

A daily apple is good for you because it helps build your immune system.

THE HEALTH BENEFITS OF THE FRUIT HAVE BEEN KNOWN FOR GENERATIONS. AN 1866 PUBLICATION SAID, "EAT AN APPLE ON GOING TO BED, AND YOU'LL KEEP THE DOCTOR FROM EARNING HIS BREAD."

The apple contains all sorts of healthy things. It's an excellent source of pectin, a form of fiber that lowers blood pressure and levels of glucose (sugar) and LDL, or "bad" cholesterol, in the body. Pectin is good for maintaining the digestive system.

Apples have other important nutrients as well.

And don't forget that when you eat an apple, it acts like a toothbrush, because it cleans teeth and kills bacteria in your mouth, which can reduce the risk of tooth decay.

HOW DO YOU LIKE THEM APPLES?

- More than 7,500 varieties of apples are grown in the world, including 2,500 varieties in the United States.
- Red Delicious is the most popular and most-produced apple in America. Golden Delicious is the second most popular.
- The only apple native to North America is the crab apple.
- Washington, New York, Michigan, Pennsylvania, and California are the top five apple-producing states.

FACT or FAKE?
BREAD CRUST is better for you than the other part of the bread.

Crust is good for you.

IF YOU'RE A PICKY EATER WHO CUTS OFF THE CRUST FROM YOUR BOLOGNA SANDWICH BEFORE EATING, YOU MIGHT WANT TO RECONSIDER. The crust contains more antioxidants than the rest of the bread.

A study published in the American Chemical Society's *Journal of Agricultural and Food Chemistry* says bread crust contains not only powerful antioxidants that can combat cancer, but also dietary fiber that can prevent colon cancer.

So, go ahead and eat the crust. And by the way, nutritionists recommend that you eat whole-wheat bread, because it's loaded with more nutrients than most breads.

JUST LOAFIN'

Here are just a few superstitions and legends about bread:

- Having a piece of bread in the baby's cradle will keep the infant healthy.
- Buttered bread will always land buttered-side down.
- If a boy and girl eat from the same loaf, they will fall in love.
- It is bad luck to turn a loaf of bread upside down or cut an unbaked loaf.
- Cutting bread in an uneven manner is a sign that you have been telling lies.
- To dream of bread means happy events to come.

FACT or FAKE?

CHEWING GUM stays in your stomach for up to seven years.

If you swallow gum, it won't stay in your stomach for long.

GUM WILL PASS THROUGH YOUR DIGESTIVE SYSTEM WITHIN A FEW DAYS IN PRETTY MUCH THE SAME CONDITION AS WHEN YOU WERE CHEWING IT.

Gum is generally made up of four basic ingredients—flavorings, sweeteners, softeners, and a combination of synthetic chemicals that make up the chewy base. The acids and enzymes in your stomach and intestines easily break down the gum's first three ingredients. But the chewy gum base is sturdy because it's designed to resist the digestive properties of the saliva in your mouth. Even so, it's no match for your digestive system. Although the gastric juices might not break down the gum base, your body will recognize it as useless food and push it out of you like any other waste product.

STICKING TO THE FACTS

- Americans chew an average of 182 sticks of gum per year. In the United Kingdom, it's 125 sticks; Germany, 103; Russia, 84; China, 20; and India, 4.
- More than 374 trillion sticks of chewing gum are made every year.
- More than one third of all chewing gum is manufactured by the Wrigley Company.
- Singapore has banned chewing gum for its citizens.
- The very first bubble gum was invented by Frank Henry Fleer in 1906. He called it Blibber-Blubber.

FACT or FAKE?
SUGAR makes kids hyperactive.

Here's good news if you have a sweet tooth: The link between sugar and hyperactivity doesn't exist.

PEDIATRICIAN AARON CARROLL OF THE RILEY HOSPITAL FOR CHILDREN AT INDIANA UNIVERSITY HEALTH EXAMINED TWELVE PUBLISHED STUDIES ON THIS SUBJECT—AND ALL OF THEM CAME UP WITH THE SAME RESULT: THERE WAS NO DIFFERENCE IN BEHAVIOR BETWEEN CHILDREN WHO CONSUMED SWEETS AND THOSE WHO DIDN'T. This mythical connection between sugar and kids' wildness is "entirely in parents' heads," Dr. Carroll wrote in the *Incidental Economist*.

"In my favorite of these studies, children were divided into two groups," said Dr. Carroll. "All of them were given a sugar-free beverage to drink. But half the parents were told that their child had just had a drink with sugar. Then, all of the parents were told to grade their children's behavior. Not surprisingly, the parents of children who thought their children had drunk a ton of sugar rated their children as significantly more hyperactive."

So why do some kids seem to turn into maniacs when they consume an abundance of sugar?

"When kids are having fun at birthday parties, on holidays, and at family celebrations, sugar-laden food is frequently served," explains Tim Crow, associate professor of nutrition at Deakin University in Australia. "It's the fun, freedom, and contact with other kids that makes them hyperactive, not the food they consume."

FACT or FAKE?

You shouldn't eat an **EGG** if it floats in a bowl of water.

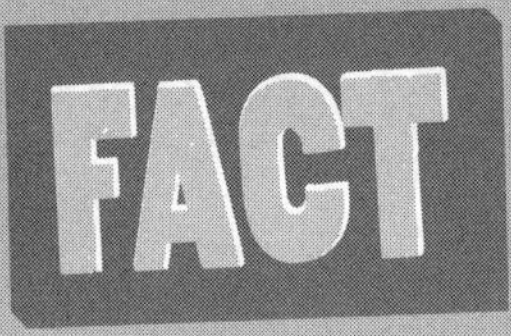

One of the worst odors you'll ever smell in the kitchen is a rotten egg. So how do you know if an egg is bad without cracking it open? See if it floats.

EVERY EGG HAS A LITTLE SPACE FILLED WITH AIR THAT RESIDES INSIDE THE FLATTER, BOTTOM PART OF THE SHELL. The size of this air pocket will determine how buoyant (floatable) the egg will be. As the egg gets older and loses freshness, its membrane separates inside the shell, allowing for a larger pocket of air.

One common way to determine an egg's freshness is to try the float test. Fill a bowl with cold water and carefully place the egg in it. A fresh egg will lie on the bottom of the bowl. An egg that is a week or two old will still remain at the bottom but might stand on end or bob below the surface. By three weeks old, the large end of the egg will go bottom up, pointing to the surface. A rotten egg will float on the top of the water.

Although this method isn't perfect, it's the most reliable, and one that has been used for generations.

EGGS-ELLENT FACTS

- In modern henhouses, most eggs are laid between seven and eleven A.M.
- A hen requires about twenty-four to twenty-six hours to produce an egg.
- The U.S. produces about seventy-five billion eggs a year.
- About 60 percent of the eggs in the U.S. are used by consumers and about 9 percent are used by the food-service industry. The rest are turned into egg products by manufacturers to make foods such as mayonnaise and cake mixes.

FACT or FAKE?

A **TURKEY** dinner makes you sleepier than any other meal.

You know how some people start nodding off after Thanksgiving dinner? They want to blame their drowsiness on the turkey. Well, it's not the bird's fault. They get sleepy because they ate too much of *everything*.

TURKEY CONTAINS AN AMINO ACID CALLED TRYPTOPHAN THAT IS ASSOCIATED WITH SLEEPINESS, SO EATING SLICES OF THAT JUICY MEAT WILL PUT SOME TRYPTOPHAN IN YOUR BLOODSTREAM. But turkey doesn't even crack the top fifty in a list of tryptophan-rich foods. Spinach, crab, shrimp, lobster, and duck all have more of the amino acid than turkey has. Foods such as tuna, chicken, and pork have nearly the same levels as turkey.

Even if you skipped the turkey on Thanksgiving, the side dishes alone could make you sleepy. That's because the real culprits are the carbohydrates, such as mashed potatoes, bread stuffing, candied yams, and dinner rolls. Studies show that carbohydrate-rich meals trigger the pancreas to release insulin, the hormone that helps you utilize sugar. This sets off a chemical process in your body that ultimately makes you sleepy. And don't forget that eating more than you normally do—which often happens on the holidays—can also make you want to doze off.

FACT or FAKE?

More **PIZZA** is delivered on New Year's Eve than at any other time of the year.

The biggest day for pizza delivery is on Super Bowl Sunday.

"PIZZA HAS BECOME TO SUPER BOWL SUNDAY WHAT EGGS ARE TO EASTER. Or candy canes to Christmas," says *USA Today*. According to a poll by Jacent Technologies, 62 percent of those questioned said they are most likely to order pizza during the Super Bowl.

An estimated forty-eight to fifty million Americans order takeout or delivery food while watching the game, according to the National Restaurant Association. Of those customers, more than 60 percent order pizza. About half the customers also order chicken wings and 20 percent get sandwiches.

Pizza.com says that besides Super Bowl Sunday, the other biggest pizza-eating days, in order, are New Year's Eve, Halloween, the night before Thanksgiving, and New Year's Day.

FACT or FAKE?

DOUBLE-DIPPING—sticking a potato chip back into a bowl of dip after taking a bite—will contaminate the whole bowl.

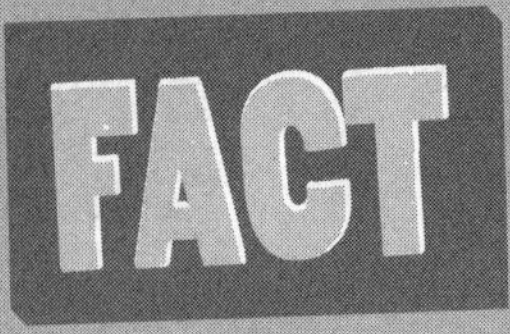

You might think twice about sampling that salsa after seeing someone double-dip, because that person likely contaminated the whole bowl.

A CLEMSON UNIVERSITY STUDY OF DOUBLE-DIPPING CHIPS INTO BOWLS OF SALSA, CHEESE DIP, AND CHOCOLATE SYRUP REVEALED THAT THIS ETIQUETTE GAFFE IS NOT ONLY GROSS BUT UNHEALTHY. Researchers found that, on average, three to six double-dips transferred about ten thousand bacteria from the eater's mouth to the remaining dip.

The salsa picked up more bacteria than the cheese or chocolate because it was runny. The thicker dips stuck to the chip more, and so there were fewer bacteria left behind in the bowl.

DO YOU DOUBLE-DIP?

CNN asked its viewers, "Do you double-dip?" Here are the results:

- 37 percent: Eeeeewwww! No, and I won't eat after I see people do it.
- 25 percent: Yes. Life is too short to worry about such things.
- 16 percent: Only if there are one or two other people.
- 7 percent: I have, but I see the error of my ways.
- 7 percent: I refuse to eat communal (shared) food.
- 6 percent: No, but I'll still eat after I have seen people do it.
- 2 percent: Other answers.

FACT or FAKE?

You can get **WARTS** from handling toads.

You get warts from being in contact with viruses, not from playing with toads.

THE MYTH PROBABLY HAS SURVIVED FOR CENTURIES BECAUSE OF THE WAY TOADS LOOK. They have rough, bumpy skin with glands that look like warts. These "warts" are really mucus glands and poison glands. When a toad is alarmed or feels threatened, its glands release a milky liquid.

Some toads are poisonous, but they don't give you warts.

Warts are caused by a common virus called HPV (short for human papillomavirus) that's spread through close contact with other people. It enters the skin through cuts or scratches, causing the cells to multiply rapidly. Because warts are slightly contagious, it's best not to touch someone else's wart. Scientists say that three out of every four persons will get a wart at some time in their lives.

Handling a common toad or frog is harmless, but it's a good idea to wash your hands once you're done holding it. The only time you need to worry about touching a frog or toad is if you encounter the South American poison dart frog. The tiny, colorful amphibian secretes a powerful poison that can kill you.

FACT or FAKE?

READING in the dark will not ruin your eyesight.

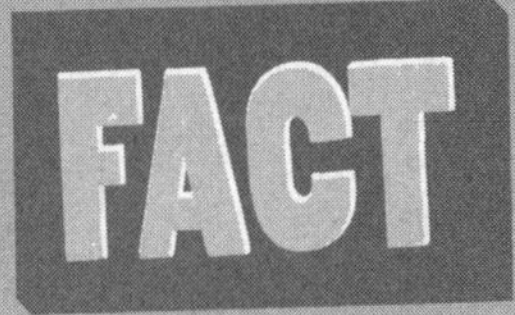

It's okay to read in the dark.

IF YOU'VE EVER BEEN CAUGHT LATE AT NIGHT READING A BOOK UNDER THE COVERS WITH A FLASHLIGHT, YOU PROBABLY HEARD MOM WARN THAT YOU'LL RUIN YOUR VISION. The next time she says that, you can say that studies show reading in the dark might strain your eyes and give you a headache, but it won't cause lasting damage.

Low light conditions make it more difficult to read in the dark because our ability to see fine detail is reduced. It will cause eye fatigue or eyestrain, but this is only a temporary discomfort. Reading in poor light will not hurt your eyes.

Most people will experience some decline in their vision as they age. How much your eyes weaken over decades is determined by family history more than any other single factor, according to genetic research.

IN THE BLINK OF AN EYE

- Your eyes blink as much as 12 times a minute; 720 times an hour; and 11,520 times a day (assuming you get eight hours of sleep). That's more than 4.2 million times a year!
- When you blink, you shut your eyes for 0.3 seconds.
- Blinking helps to wash tears over your eyeballs. That keeps them clean and moist. Also, if something is about to hit your eye, you will blink automatically.
- It's impossible to sneeze without blinking or closing your eyes.

FACT or FAKE?

You shouldn't suck on a snakebite to remove the **POISON.**

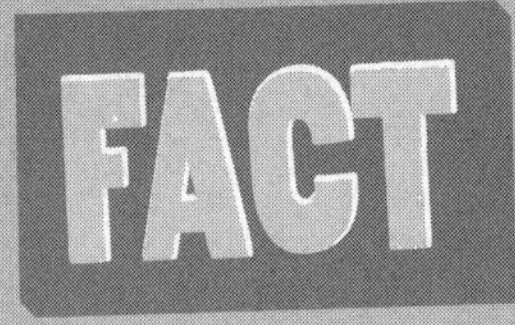

You might have seen an old Western where the hero cuts open his buddy's snakebite and sucks out the poison. If you were to do that today, you would probably make things a lot worse for the victim.

THE "CUT-AND-SUCK" METHOD HAS NEVER BEEN PROVEN EFFECTIVE, ACCORDING TO STUDIES. Because venom spreads so quickly in the body, it's unlikely that you can suck much of it out. Also, about 20 percent of snakebites totally lack venom. Cutting into the skin creates a nasty wound and increases the risk of infection.

So what should you do? Get away from the snake but try to remember its appearance such as color, markings, and shape of head. This can prove helpful when the victim is being treated in the emergency room. If you have a cell phone, call 911. Keep the bitten person still and calm. Lay or sit the person down so that the bite is below the level of the heart. Wash the bite area with soap and water and cover it with a clean, dry dressing. Remove any jewelry or tight-fitting clothing in case of swelling. Mark the edge of any swollen area every fifteen minutes with a pen. This helps doctors judge the extent of the poisoning.

SNAKES ALIVE!

- On average, poisonous snakes bite seven to eight thousand people a year in the United States. About five or six victims die.
- If you're hiking, wear high-cut boots to protect your ankles. Watch where you put your hands and feet, especially when scrambling on rocky ledges or gathering wood.
- It should go without saying: Do not approach, poke, pick up, or otherwise harass a snake. Two-thirds of bites happen to people who are intentionally messing with the reptile.

FACT or FAKE?

Sitting too close to the **TV** will ruin your eyesight.

Sitting closer than necessary to the television or a computer monitor might give you a headache, but it won't damage your vision.

SINCE THE 1950S, PARENTS HAVE BEEN CAUTIONING THEIR KIDS NOT TO SIT TOO CLOSE TO THE TV SET FOR FEAR THEY WOULD RUIN THEIR EYESIGHT. At one time it was true, because of the radiation coming from old TV sets. But thanks to today's technology, that warning is no longer valid.

The first TV sets sent out radiation levels that could have heightened the risk of eye problems in some people who consistently sat too close. Back then it was wise for Mom to insist that everyone stay far enough away. Radiation isn't a factor anymore because modern televisions have protective shielding.

Although it's unlikely you will suffer any eye damage by staring at the screen for long periods, you might end up with eyestrain. To avoid this, keep the room well-lit while spending time in front of the TV or computer monitor and move your eyes away from the screen every so often.

FACT or FAKE?

Listening to **LOUD MUSIC** can cause permanent hearing loss.

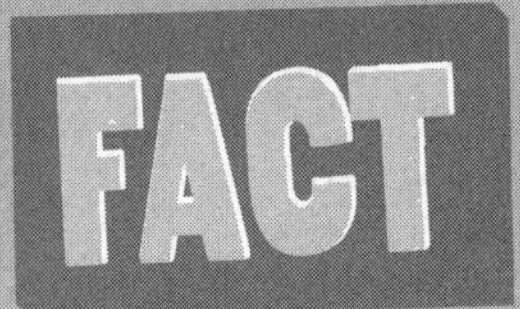

You might want to turn down your MP3 player or iPod, because playing it too loudly can cause permanent damage to your hearing.

WHEN YOU ARE EXPOSED TO HARMFUL NOISE—MUSIC THAT IS PLAYED TOO LOUD AND FOR TOO LONG—SENSITIVE STRUCTURES IN YOUR INNER EAR CAN BE DAMAGED, CAUSING NOISE-INDUCED HEARING LOSS. These sensitive structures, called hair cells, are small sensory nerve endings that convert sound energy into electrical signals that travel to the brain. Once damaged, your hair cells cannot grow back.

Sound is measured in units called decibels. Normal conversation is about 60 decibels, while motorcycles, firecrackers, and small firearms range from 120 to 150 decibels. Music from headphones and earbuds at maximum volume are about 110 decibels, while a rock concert is between 120 and 140. Long or repeated exposure to sounds at or above 85 decibels can cause hearing loss, warns the National Institute on Deafness and Other Communication Disorders.

Continuous exposure to loud music can cause not only gradual hearing loss but also tinnitus—a ringing, roaring, or buzzing in the ears or head.

Sounds of less than 75 decibels, even after long exposure, are unlikely to cause hearing loss.

FACT or FAKE?

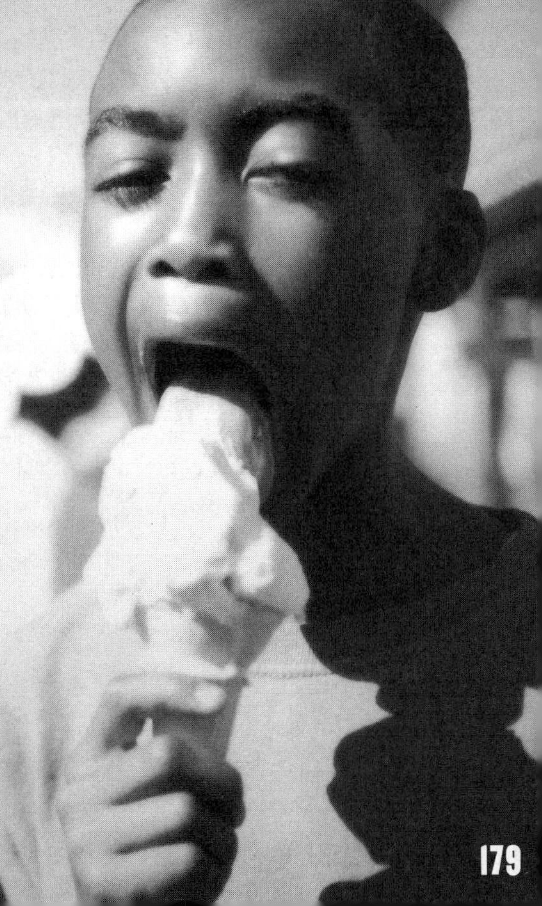

BRAIN FREEZE is a real but temporary medical condition.

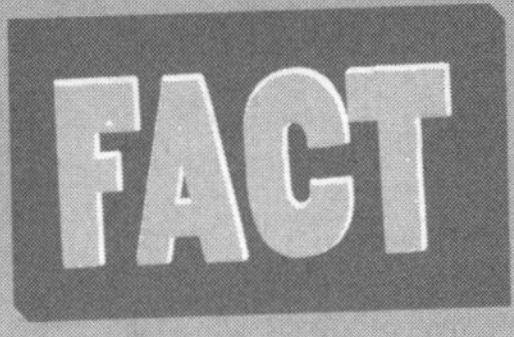

Got an instant headache after swallowing an ice-cold treat? You just suffered a medical condition called *sphenopalatine ganglioneuralgia*. We know it as "brain freeze."

HERE'S WHAT HAPPENS: WHEN AN ICE-COLD DRINK TOUCHES THE ROOF OF YOUR MOUTH, THE BLOOD VESSELS SHRINK. Almost immediately, the tiny vessels begin to expand again, allowing blood to rush back in to warm up your mouth. It's like when your cheeks turn a rosy color after spending a long time outside in the winter. The headache that follows when you consume something cold is triggered when the pain receptors in your mouth signal your brain. That results in a sharp but fleeting pain in your forehead.

The best way to avoid brain freeze is simply to eat slower and let the cold drink or treat melt in your mouth before swallowing. If you do get a brain freeze, the best way to minimize or shorten it is to press your tongue against the roof of your mouth or drink something warm.

FACT or FAKE?

Swimming less than an hour after you eat can cause **CRAMPS** and lead to drowning.

It's a myth that you have to wait thirty minutes or even an hour until you can swim after eating.

YOUR BODY IS FULLY CAPABLE OF PROVIDING ENOUGH OXYGEN TO YOUR STOMACH AND YOUR LIMBS WHEN YOU SWIM RIGHT AFTER YOU EAT, AS LONG AS YOU DIDN'T GORGE YOURSELF.

The simple fact is that a full stomach does not significantly impact your ability to swim. Scientists say that although blood rushes to the stomach to aid in the digestion process after you eat, it is not nearly enough blood to cause your muscles to lose energy and their ability to perform.

According to the Centers for Disease Control, about 3,500 people drown each year in the United States. Of those victims, virtually none drown because they have just eaten.

Although swimming right after eating a light meal won't harm you, it's probably a good idea to wait a little bit if you wolfed down a big dinner.

To get the best results when **EXERCISING**, follow the rule "No pain, no gain."

Although there's nothing wrong with a vigorous workout, there's no need to work through the pain. In fact, experts say, you can do yourself more harm than good.

OF ALL THE FITNESS MYTHS THAT HAVE SURFACED, EXPERTS AGREE THAT THE "NO PAIN, NO GAIN" BELIEF IS DANGEROUS. Certainly, you might be a little sore after an intense exercise routine, but you shouldn't be in pain while you are working out.

Celebrity fitness trainer Harley Pasternak told the *Today Show*, "Many people think if their muscles don't hurt, they're not having a quality workout. This is way off base. While resistance training can be intense, and some level of discomfort may occur, pain is not required for a successful workout. It's also important to note that pain can be a warning sign of an exhausted muscle or torn ligament."

If you are experiencing pain during a fitness activity, either you are doing it wrong, or you already have an injury. In either case, stop, rest, and wait for the pain to go away. If it doesn't, or if it gets worse while exercising, see a doctor.

ODDS AND ENDS

Pirates' number one **PUNISHMENT** was making the troublemaker walk the plank.

Most pirate movies you've seen probably had someone walking the plank. In reality, this form of execution was seldom used.

WHEN PIRATES WANTED TO PUNISH SOMEONE WITH DEATH, THEY SIMPLY THREW HIM OVERBOARD . . . OR SHOT HIM.

"Pirates preferred to not kill their victims," says Dr. Karl Kruszelnicki, of the University of Sydney. "After all, if people thought that pirates would always kill their captives, they would fight to the death. As a result, in one case, the pirate Thomas Tew, with a crew of just forty, attacked a ship carrying three hundred heavily armed soldiers, who surrendered to the forty pirates. Second, if they had to kill, pirates would usually dispatch their enemies as quickly and unromantically as possible."

Although walking the plank was an extremely rare form of execution, the myth that pirates often resorted to this punishment gained popularity in the late nineteenth century with the publication of Robert Louis Stevenson's classic *Treasure Island*, and other books about pirates.

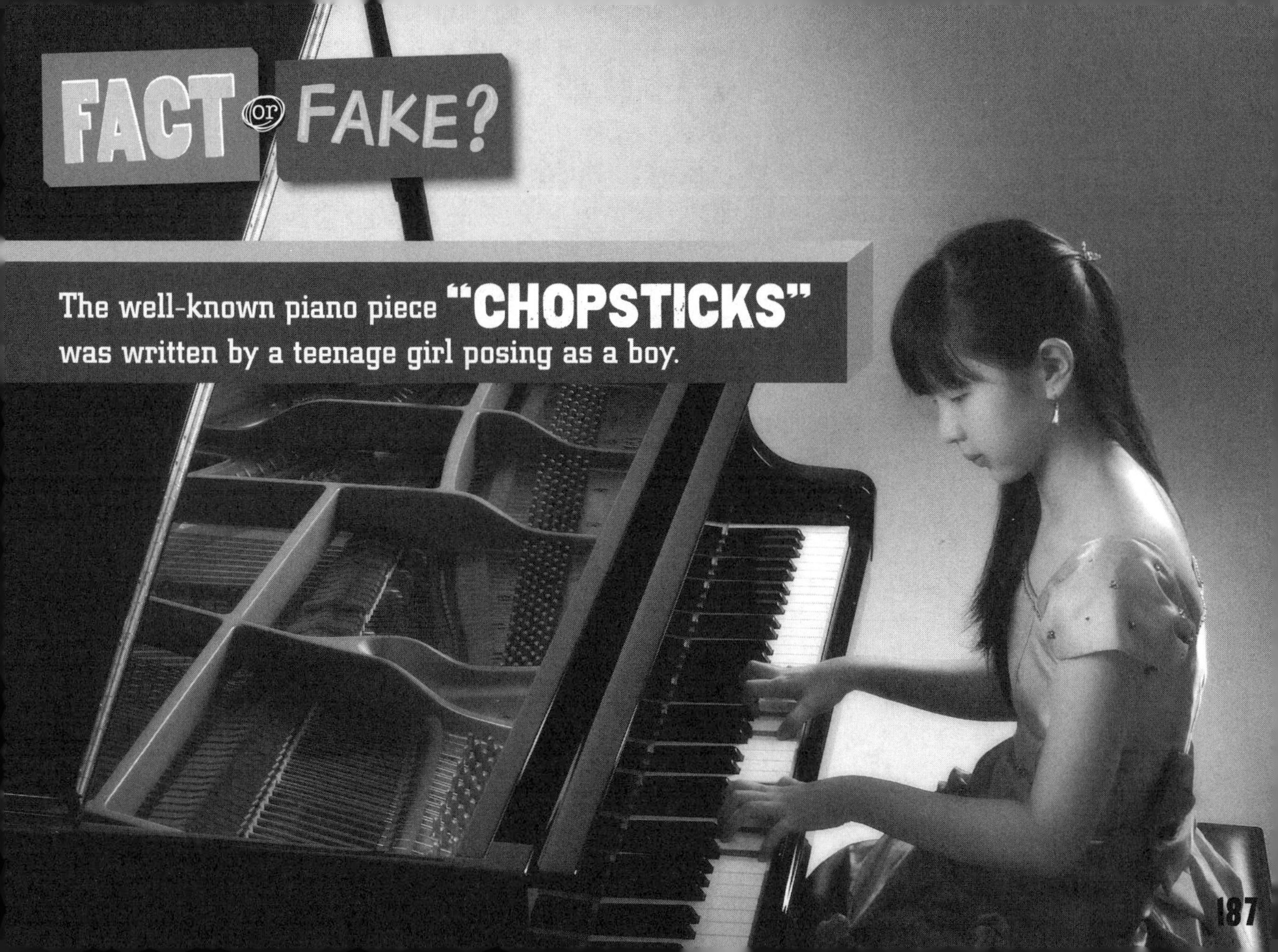

FACT or FAKE?

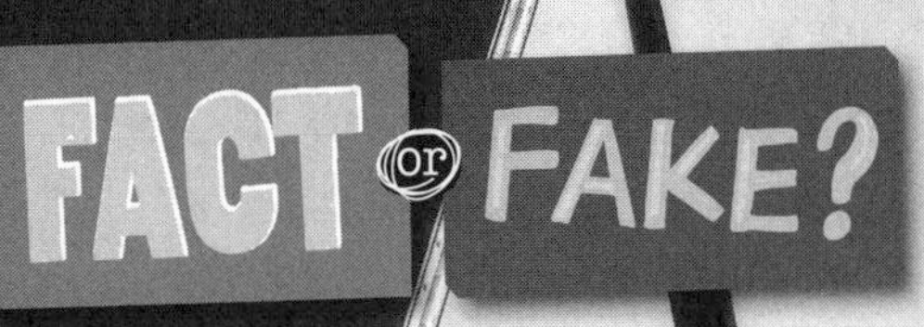

The well-known piano piece **"CHOPSTICKS"** was written by a teenage girl posing as a boy.

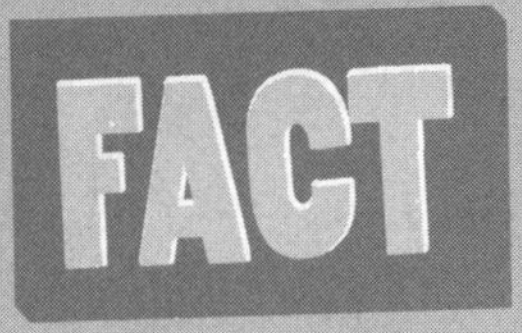

One of the first songs anyone ever plays on the piano was written by sixteen-year-old Euphemia Allen, who composed the piece under the fake name Arthur de Lulli.

THE BRITISH GIRL WAS THE SISTER OF A MUSIC PUBLISHER WHEN SHE WROTE THE PIECE IN 1877 AND CALLED IT "THE CELEBRATED CHOP WALTZ ARRANGED AS A DUET AND SOLO FOR THE PIANO-FORTE."

She wanted pianists to play her piece as if they were karate-chopping the keys. On page three of the sheet music were these instructions: "This part . . . must be played with both hands turned sideways, the little fingers lowest, so that the movements of the hands imitate the chopping from which this waltz gets its name."

The tune, which was first performed in London, England, and Glasgow, Scotland, became a favorite of piano beginners, and has been passed down for generations as "Chopsticks."

HOW THE PIANO GOT ITS NAME

An Italian musical instrument builder named Bartolomeo Cristofori invented the piano in Florence, Italy, in 1700. His invention is considered the first practical piano because it contained a mechanism for the hammers to strike the strings in such a way that it could be played loudly and softly. Cristofori's original name for his invention was the *piano et forte,* which means "soft and loud" in Italian. It was eventually shortened to *piano.*

When you open your parachute while **SKYDIVING**, you momentarily go back up.

You do not go back up when you open your parachute.

IF YOU WATCH A VIDEO OF A SKYDIVER AT THE MOMENT HIS PARACHUTE IS DEPLOYED, IT LOOKS LIKE HE'S JERKED BACK UP FOR A FEW SECONDS. But it's an optical illusion. He and the videographer both are falling; it's just that the videographer is falling faster until his own chute opens.

The typical skydiver jumps out of airplanes at an altitude of 12,500 feet and reaches speeds of about 115 miles an hour, enjoying a freefall for about one minute before deploying the parachute at a "pull altitude" of 2,000 to 2,500 feet. Experienced skydivers falling in a heads-down vertical position known as free-flying can reach speeds of more than 200 miles an hour.

When the rip cord is pulled, the main parachute (assuming it's been properly packed) will fully deploy after the skydiver has fallen several hundred additional feet. You don't want the chute to open too quickly, because you will feel an unpleasant jerk. But no matter what, when the chute opens, you don't go back up. You're still falling.

FACT or FAKE?

James Earl Jones, the voice of **DARTH VADER,** refused to have his name in the credits of the first two *Star Wars* films.

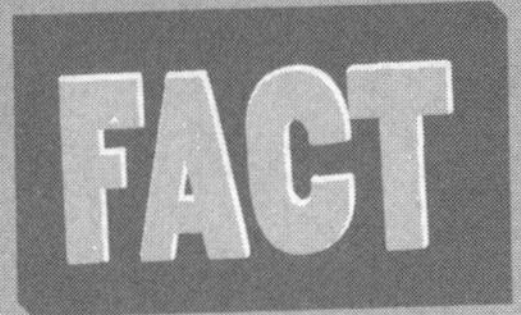

James Earl Jones chose not to have his name on the credits of the original *Star Wars* movie in 1977 and the 1980 sequel, *The Empire Strikes Back*.

JAMES EARL JONES DID THE VOICE OF DARTH VADER—THE JEDI KNIGHT WHO TURNED TO THE DARK SIDE OF THE FORCE. But Vader was played in costume by English bodybuilder David Prowse, whose voice wasn't deep or strong enough to suit the film's creator, George Lucas. Jones was hired to dub Vader's dialogue during postproduction.

Jones said he didn't think he was worthy of credit because he supplied only the voice of the character. He thought his voice should be considered nothing more than a special effect. But Jones's distinctive, resonating voice was so linked to Vader's character that the actor agreed to be credited in the third *Star Wars* film, *Return of the Jedi*, in 1983.

Jones was later credited in the first two *Star Wars* films when they were re-released in 1997.

The creators of **SUPERMAN** became millionaires when they sold the rights to DC Comics.

Fresh out of high school, writer Jerry Siegel and artist Joe Shuster created Superman and sold it to DC Comics for a paltry $130 in 1939.

SIEGEL AND SHUSTER SPENT THE REST OF THEIR LIVES TRYING TO GET BACK THE RIGHTS TO WHAT HAS BECOME A BILLION-DOLLAR FRANCHISE.

In the era when the Man of Steel was introduced to the public, it was standard practice in the comic book industry for the creators to sign away all rights to their characters, which Siegel and Shuster did. DC Comics hired the pair as staff members, paying them $10 per comic book page. Nine years later, with Superman one of the most popular comic book heroes of all time, Siegel and Shuster were each making only $35 a page.

In 1948, the pair sued DC for the rights to Superman. They lost in court but settled in a related case for $100,000. The creators didn't give up the fight, and eventually Warner Communications, which owned DC Comics, agreed to give the men $20,000 a year each. Sadly, they both died broke.

SUPER FACTS

- Superman was born on the planet Krypton to Lara and Jor-El, who named him Kal-El, which means "star-child."
- Sent to Earth shortly before Krypton blew up, he was raised as Clark Joseph Kent by his adoptive parents, Kansas farmers Jonathan and Martha Kent.
- The famous *S* shield on his Superman outfit is really a Kryptonian symbol that means "hope."

FACT or FAKE?
Fishing is the most DANGEROUS occupation in the United States.

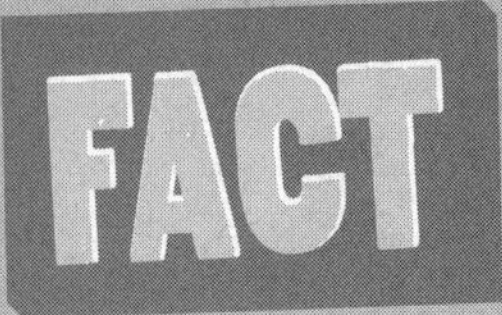

Fishing offshore on a charter boat or pleasure craft is fun, but for those who fish for a living, it can be dangerous.

AS A LIVELIHOOD, FISHING HAS BEEN THE MOST HAZARDOUS JOB IN AMERICA EVERY YEAR SINCE 1992.

Fishers, as they are called, work at an occupation that is six times more deadly than being a law-enforcement officer.

"Fishers and related fishing workers often work under hazardous conditions, and transportation to a hospital or doctor often is not readily available when injuries do occur," the Bureau of Labor Statistics says. "The crew must guard against the danger of injury from malfunctioning fishing gear, entanglement in fishing nets and gear, slippery decks, ice formation, or large waves washing over the deck." Fishers also must contend with dangerous fog, high seas, and storms.

DANGER ZONE

Here are the fatality rates per one hundred thousand workers of the country's most hazardous jobs in 2011:

- Fishers, 121
- Log workers, 102
- Airplane pilots and flight engineers, 57
- Sanitation workers, 41
- Roofers, 31
- Steel workers, 26
- Farmers and ranchers, 25
- Truck drivers and deliverers, 24
- Power-line installers and repairers, 20
- Taxi drivers and chauffers, 19

FACT or FAKE?

BLACK BOXES in planes are not black.

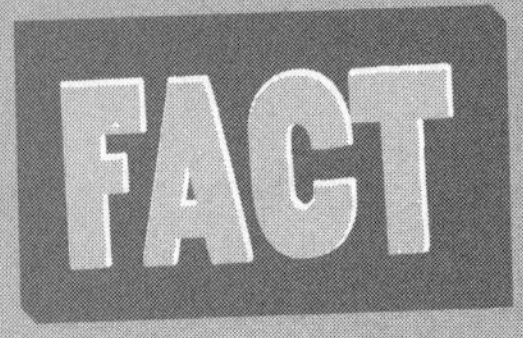

An airplane's nearly indestructible device that provides vital flight information in case of a crash is called the "black box," which is odd, because it's really bright orange.

THE BLACK BOX CONTAINS TWO KINDS OF RECORDERS. THE FLIGHT DATA RECORDER KEEPS TRACK OF THE AIRCRAFT'S OPERATING CONDITIONS, SUCH AS ALTITUDE, AIRSPEED, AND FUEL FLOW. The cockpit voice recorder tapes cockpit conversations and radio communications. This recorder is on a thirty-minute-long loop, so if the plane crashes, the last thirty minutes before impact have been recorded.

Located in the tail section of the airplane, the device is carefully engineered and constructed to withstand a high-speed impact and intense fire following a crash. The information the recorders gather is stored within the device on a crash-survivable memory unit protected by a titanium-cast shell. To help crash investigators find the device in the wreckage, the outside of the black box is coated in heat-resistant, reflective, bright orange paint.

SO WHY IS IT CALLED A BLACK BOX?

The inventor was an Australian aeronautical engineer, Dr. David Warren. According to the Powerhouse Museum in Sydney, "'black box' is a metaphor for a device whose workings we don't understand or need to understand, but whose output is interesting." There are other theories about its name, including that it's a reference to death or because it's covered in ashes after a crash.

Most **VIDEO GAMES** are played by kids.

Video games are hardly for kids. Nearly 70 percent of all gamers are adults.

ACCORDING TO THE ENTERTAINMENT SOFTWARE ASSOCIATION (ESA), THE AVERAGE GAMER IS THIRTY YEARS OLD AND HAS BEEN PLAYING FOR TWELVE YEARS. Sixty-eight percent of gamers are eighteen years of age or older.

Forty-seven percent of all players are women, which make up one of the industry's fastest growing groups. In fact, says the ESA, adult women represent a greater portion of the game-playing population (30 percent) than boys ages seventeen or younger (18 percent).

Some other facts from the ESA: Sixty-two percent of gamers play games with others, either in person or online. Seventy-eight percent of these gamers play with others at least one hour per week. Thirty-three percent of gamers play social games. Many gamers play on the go: Thirty-three percent play games on their smartphones, and twenty-five percent play on their handheld device.

PLUGGED IN

Kids ages eight to eighteen spend 53 hours a week with their electronic media, including cell phones, video games, computers, iPods, and TV, according to a 2010 study by the Kaiser Family Foundation. Among other findings:

- Kids spend an average of 7 hours and 38 minutes a day using electronic media.
- 66 percent have their own cell phones.
- 76 percent have their own iPods or MP3 players.
- 20 percent of kids' media comes from mobile devices.
- 47 percent still find time to read books.

FACT or FAKE?

PLAY-DOH was originally designed as wallpaper cleaner.

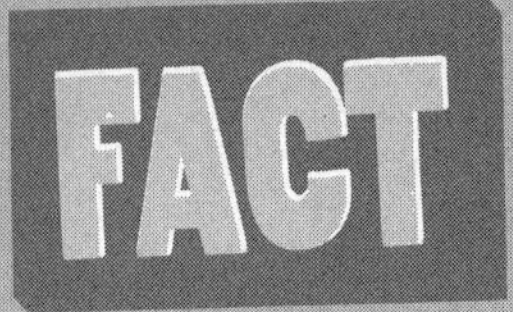

One of little kids' most popular playthings started out as a substance for cleaning wallpaper.

IN 1955, BROTHERS NOAH AND JOSEPH McVICKER INVENTED A COMPOUND MADE OUT OF FLOUR, SALT, WATER, BORIC ACID, AND SILICON OIL. When rolled against wallpaper, it cleaned off any dust and soot.

But later that year, Joseph McVicker heard a teacher complaining that classroom clay was too difficult for many of the smaller children to mold. Figuring his new wallpaper cleaner would make the perfect substitute for modeling clay, he shipped a box to the school. It became an instant hit, so he supplied other schools in the Cincinnati area with this new material. After great reactions from teachers and students, McVicker called his product Play-Doh and sold it purely as a plaything. Back then, it came in only one color—beige—but was eventually sold in red, yellow, blue, and many other colors.

Today more than two billion cans of Play-Doh have been sold–and probably just as many pieces of the stuff have been found in carpets, clothes, and furniture.

FACT or FAKE?
ROBIN HOOD was England's most sought-after criminal of all time.

Despite years of research, there is absolutely no evidence that a real-life Robin Hood—an archer, swordsman, and outlaw who stole from the rich and gave to the poor—ever existed.

THE ADVENTURES OF THE HERO AND HIS FELLOW OUTLAWS, KNOWN AS HIS "MERRY MEN," WERE FIRST TOLD IN BALLADS AND MADE-UP TALES OF REAL CRIMINALS DURING THE MIDDLE AGES (FIFTH TO THE FIFTEENTH CENTURY) IN ENGLAND.

The earliest surviving text of a Robin Hood ballad is called "Robin Hood and the Monk," which was written around 1450. Preserved at Cambridge University, the ballad tells the tale of how Robin Hood was captured by the corrupt sheriff of Nottingham. But Robin's second-in-command, Little John, helps the outlaw escape. Then they steal much of the tax money that the sheriff had stolen from the people.

For centuries afterward, the legend of Robin Hood and his band of Merry Men from Sherwood Forest continued to grow in songs, books, films, and television.

FACT or FAKE?
King Tut's CURSE caused the deaths of all those who broke into his tomb.

The mummy's curse was much more fiction than fact.

IN 1922, AFTER A FIFTEEN-YEAR SEARCH, ARCHAEOLOGIST HOWARD CARTER AND HIS TEAM OPENED A STUNNING TOMB IN EGYPT'S VALLEY OF THE KINGS—THAT OF THE PHARAOH TUTANKHAMUN. Allegedly, inside the tomb, one of Carter's men found a clay tablet that read: "Death will slay with his wings whoever disturbs the peace of the pharaoh." Soon, more than two dozen men in Carter's party began to die off, having fallen victim to the curse. After seeing all his friends and associates and pets die, Carter then died himself.

It makes for a great story. But that's all it is—just a wild tale perpetrated by sensationalist newspapers at the time. Only two members of the expedition died shortly after the tomb was breached. Carter's good friend George Herbert, who had been in frail health, died four months afterward from an infected mosquito bite, and George Jay Gould, who helped bankroll the expedition, died five months afterward from a high fever. Carter died nearly seventeen years later at the age of sixty-four.

In 2002, the *British Medical Journal* published a study by Dr. Mark Nelson, of Monash University in Australia, concerning the deaths of Carter and his party. The twenty-five westerners exposed to the "curse" lived to an average age of seventy. Nelson concluded there was "no evidence to support the existence of a mummy's curse."

ABOUT THE AUTHOR

ALLAN ZULLO IS THE AUTHOR OF MORE THAN 100 NONFICTION BOOKS ON SUBJECTS RANGING FROM SPORTS AND THE SUPERNATURAL TO HISTORY AND ANIMALS.

He has written the bestselling Haunted Kids series, published by Scholastic, which is filled with chilling stories based on, or inspired by, documented cases from the files of ghost hunters. Allan also has introduced Scholastic readers to the Ten True Tales series, about people—especially kids—who have met the challenges of dangerous, sometimes life-threatening, situations.

Allan, the grandfather of five and the father of two grown daughters, lives with his wife, Kathryn, on the side of a mountain near Asheville, North Carolina. To learn more about the author, visit his website at www.allanzullo.com.

RATE YOUR  I.Q.!

HOW MANY OF THE 100 STATEMENTS DID YOU CORRECTLY IDENTIFY AS EITHER FACT OR FICTION?

CORRECT ANSWERS	RANK
90 TO 100	**Outstanding** You are a Human Truth Detector—and that's a fact!
75 TO 89	**Excellent** You are no phony in separating fact from fiction.
50 TO 74	**Good** You usually know the difference between myth and reality.
25 TO 49	**Okay** You may find it difficult to recognize a true tale from a tall tale.
0 TO 24	**Rookie** You'll do better next time—and that's the truth!